The
Ancient Love Song

N   :H

The *Ancient Love Song*

Finding Christ in the Old Testament

Charles D. Drew

Foreword by Edmund P. Clowney

P U B L I S H I N G
P.O. BOX 817 • PHILLIPSBURG • NEW JERSEY 08865-0817

Page Design by Tobias Design
Typesetting by Michelle Feaster

Printed in the United States of America

Library of Congress Cataloging-in-Publication Data

Drew, Charles D., 1950-
      The ancient love song: finding Christ in the Old Testament /
   Charles D. Drew; foreword by Edmund P. Clowney.
            p.   cm.
      Includes bibliographical references.
      ISBN 0-87552-175-4 (pbk.)
      1. Bible. O.T.—Criticism, interpretation, etc. 2. Bible. N.T.—
   Relation to the Old Testament. 3. Jesus Christ—Person and offices—
   Biblical teaching. I. Title.

BS1171.2.D74 2000
221.6'4—dc21
                                             00-036702

CONTENTS

FOREWORD

If you love the Bible, you'll love this book. If you find the Bible rather puzzling, this book will open for you the greatest book of all. A hymn compares the Bible to a "golden casket where gems of truth are stored." I'm glad that verse doesn't stop with jewels, but concludes, "It is the heav'n-drawn picture of Christ the Living Word."

Since everyone knows that the Bible is full of gems of truth, we may be tempted to use it like the *Oxford Dictionary of Quotations* (which has a long section of famous Bible quotes). Scripture does yield a vast treasure of golden texts that are suitable for calligraphy and framing.

But the Bible is not a loose collection of verses, like some parts of the book of Proverbs. Stories fill the Bible: tales of love, like Ruth's; of courage, like David's against Goliath; of forgiveness, like Joseph's for the brothers who sold him into slavery. These stories, however, are not organized as a book of values, a collection of stories offering us good examples. The best and the brightest, like King David, can be guilty of shocking lapses, even crimes.

Rather, the Bible has one story line, featuring not great men and women, but the great and holy God. It is the story of God's saving love through the ages, and his triumph in Jesus Christ, who is Immanuel, God with us. Amazing grace is its theme, saving faith is its goal, and the Savior is its focus. Because that story was written to bring you life, you may well jump at once to the New Testament Gospels to see how it comes out. Yet the story does not begin there, and you miss much more than entertainment if you come in only for the last act.

When Jesus found Cleopas and another disciple leaving Jerusalem in shock on the very day of his resurrection, he withheld his identity and walked them through the Old Testament as he accompanied them on their journey. It was not enough to show them that he was really alive. He had to show them from the Old Testament why he died and rose again. Jesus' teaching became the heart of what the apostles also taught: "that Christ died for our sins according to the Scriptures, that he was buried, that he was raised on the third day according to the Scriptures" (1 Corinthians 15:3–4).

This book is an invitation to take a walk with Charles Drew, and, yes, with Jesus, for it is a fresh and vivid retelling of the greatest story in the world. Read it a chapter at a time, and reflect on questions that will lift your horizons. Better still, use it with a group of friends and share your discoveries. Cleopas and his friend couldn't wait! (Luke 24:32–33).

EDMUND P. CLOWNEY

PREFACE

I was strolling one afternoon in downtown Philadelphia when I noticed a young Jewish friend standing on the edge of a group of men, her eyes red with weeping. As I drew near, I discovered a rabbi and a half-dozen ardent Christians in heated discussion. It seemed that everyone was speaking at once. The "evangelists" were quoting eagerly from their Bibles, and the rabbi was countering with equal fervor. The discussion, which was already intense, grew increasingly heated until it became almost ugly. The rabbi finally shook his head and stalked angrily away.

My Jewish friend, whose tears had been over the tone of the interaction, joined me, and we followed the rabbi to a remote location where we entered into quiet conversation with him. He was very disturbed by what had happened, we learned, for two reasons. He had felt in his opponents more than a hint of anti-Semitism. And he had found their arguments unimpressive in that none of them dealt with the Old Testament in any cogent or comprehensive way.

As we spoke I considered how greatly these Philadelphia evangelists differed from the apostle Paul. For one thing, their motive seemed so different. What was for them a pitched battle was for Paul a labor of compassion. The apostle yearned for his brothers' salvation so intensely that he was prepared to be "cut off from Christ" if necessary for their sake. For another thing, Paul used the Old Testament masterfully. The Jewish scriptures were his only text, and he employed them repeatedly and at great length in the defense of the gospel. In Thessalonica he spoke all day for three Sabbaths in a row, in Ephesus he argued daily for three months, and in Corinth he spoke on every Sabbath for one and a half years. Rome heard him daily "from morning to night" for two years, roughly five thousand hours of Old Testament teaching on Christ!

Paul emulated his Master. Jesus told his enemies that the "scriptures . . . bear witness to me." On Resurrection Sunday Jesus transformed two forlorn disciples along the Emmaus road, firing their hearts with the truth that *"all* the scriptures" spoke of his suffering and glory.

The Old Testament points to Jesus in many ways. The *Law* anticipates him by exposing our hearts and persuading us of our need for a savior. The *promises* anticipate him by kindling a longing at numerous levels that only Jesus can ultimately fulfill. The *Wisdom Literature* compels us to look to him for meaning and for the ability to live wisely. Old Testament *characters* teach us to look in faith beyond the seeable world to the Messiah's eternal kingdom, and they foreshadow his great work by the role they play in Israel's life. In Old Testament *history* Christ visits his people in numerous ways, whetting our appetite for his incarnation. Old Testament *psalmists* and *prophets* often speak with the voice of Christ, anticipating his own anguish and exaltation. The Old Testament testifies to Jesus, in other words, with voices far richer and more numerous than a mere scattering of predictions (however many they may be).

We will examine in this book something of the variety and depth of this testimony. With the exception of chapter 1, which shows more fully than this preface the benefit of knowing the Old Testament well, and chapters 4 and 5, the latter of which illustrates the point of the former, this book can be read in any order. Each chapter is complete in itself.

Chapter 2 traces the unfolding of the mysterious promise in Genesis 3:15 from Genesis to Revelation. Chapter 3 shows how Christ resolves the Old Testament problem of God's closeness. Chapters 4 through 7 explore in progression how Christ is sought or revealed in Old Testament characters, in the Wisdom Literature, and in the Psalms. Those familiar with the proclamation that Christ is our Prophet, Priest, and King will recognize this in the content and order of chapters 8 through 10. Since death so often seems to have the final word in our experience, it seemed fitting to make Christ's destruction of death the subject of the final chapter.

Questions appear at the end of each chapter. Useful for either private reflection or group discussion, they aim to carry us beyond a mere review of the chapter into a deeper study of its contents. Some call for immediate personal application, and others for further Bible study. Some are fairly simple and others more complex, leading conceivably to hours of further study. Do not feel compelled to answer or discuss them all, but do tackle one or two. Such an exercise will bring the truth closer to the heart and more fully to the mind, helping to fulfill our aim to love more fully the one who has spoken with such beauty, richness, and coherence in his Word. Perhaps along the way God will equip us to declare the glory of the Messiah a little better, particularly to our Jewish friends.

Many scholars and friends have helped me in this undertaking. I am particularly grateful to the elders of Trinity Presbyterian Church in Charlottesville, Virginia, who kindly granted me the sabbatical during which I wrote the bulk of the original manuscript. Above all, my thanks and acknowledgments must go to my teacher, fellow-pastor (for a time), and friend, Edmund Clowney. His insight into the beauty of Scripture and the beauty of the One who is at its heart inspired my efforts.

Chapter 1

WHO NEEDS THE OLD TESTAMENT?

As a young couple looks on, the skywriter soars and loops through the air, writing:

Marry me Jill

As the biplane begins to spell out *Jill,* the camera pans to the face of the woman, and we watch with delight as she suddenly realizes that the message scrawled across the sky is for her. Her casual interest yields to a cry of recognition and an exuberant embrace.

I have forgotten the product that this scene was intended to advertise, but I have never forgotten the scene. What fires Jill's response, and what fills us with delight, is not just the proposal itself. It is the packaging of the proposal. The manner in which Jill's suitor makes his love known reveals how certain and deep that love is. Private promises of devotion are not enough for him. He wants the world to know. He has no interest in cheap, spur-of-the-moment declarations. Only

1

careful planning and great expense can adequately express his commitment. Jill sees this and gives her love enthusiastically to him.

How do we give our love more enthusiastically to God? In much the same way. We note the manner in which he declares his love, and we learn to wonder at the devotion of a God who would go to such great lengths in his pursuit of us.

The Old Testament is a rich and beautiful proposal of marriage, designed to win not only our faith but also our affection. Sadly, we are generally so ignorant of this packaging that our love remains unkindled. It is as if Jill were to spend the entire scene too engrossed in a brief note from her lover to look up. By the time she is done, the wind has dispersed the message, and her joy in his love is much less than it might have been.

God's Unfolding Proposal of Love

God has always loved his people. But his revelation of that love unfolds in varied fashion throughout the pages of Scripture. God begins to reveal himself and his loving plan in Genesis 3, immediately after the Fall has plunged the human race into alienation and death. Gradually over time, he reveals his loving plan with greater and greater fullness, until finally, in the fullness of time, he makes us his own spotless bride.[1]

God declares his intentions almost as soon as the Bible begins. Our first parents have just disobeyed God's command, with tragic and widespread consequences. Their re-

---

1 Galatians 4:4; Ephesians 5:25–27.

lationship with God shifts dramatically from one of love and fellowship to one of fear and guilt. Accusation and shame abruptly mark their relationship with each other. And nature, which they were designed to rule and enjoy, now becomes their mortal adversary, only grudgingly yielding food and in the end reducing them to the dust from which they came.

Astonishingly, God chooses in this distressing context to declare his love in language that contains the heart of what we have come to know as the gospel. Speaking to the Serpent (Satan), he says:

> I will put enmity between you and the woman, and between your seed and her seed; he shall bruise your head, and you shall bruise his heel.[2]

These strange words may at first seem harsh. But when we examine them more closely, we see that they are really words of great love. God is going to do something marvelous. He is going to make the woman and the Serpent hate each other. We must remember that when God first speaks these words, the woman and the Serpent are on the same team. She and her husband have just chosen to believe the Serpent's lies, and in so doing have aligned themselves and the whole human race with Satan. But God promises to intervene and rearrange things, to strip from Satan his newfound allies and make them his own again.

More marvelous still, God intends to perform this great miracle through Eve's own descendant. Her "seed" will suf-

2 Genesis 3:15 RSV.

fer at Satan's hand, but he will triumph. We do not know from this promise exactly who the descendant will be, nor are we certain if it will be an individual or a group of people. But we do know that there will be victory, and that it will come through a human being.

How comforting and humbling this great promise must have been to Eve. By listening to the Serpent, she had brought incalculable disaster upon the human race. And yet God mercifully appointed her to carry in her own womb the certain hope of restoration. He gave her a task of inestimable value.[3] We look at Eve and also take comfort. If the Lord can make her the mother of the Redeemer, then he can and will use us, no matter how far we have fallen.

"How do I love thee?" runs the old verse. "Let me count the ways." God loves us enough to restore us to himself, even though we have forfeited our right to life.[4] And he loves us enough to use us, or one like us, in the process. Such is the nature of his commitment. What unfolds from Genesis 3:15 onward is an extraordinary demonstration of that commitment. Again and again God intervenes, drawing his people back to himself, thereby reinstituting the promised enmity, until finally God himself enters history as a man, born of a woman, suffers, dies, and rises again to secure once and for all the hearts of his beloved people.

To be ignorant of this great history is to miss out. It's like being engaged without ever getting flowers or cards or un-

---

3 This high task may well be in Paul's mind in 1 Timothy 2:15, "Yet woman will be saved through bearing children" (RSV).

4 Genesis 2:17; see Romans 6:23, "For the wages of sin is death."

expected phone calls from your fiancé. You may know he loves you, but you just don't feel it. God designed the Old Testament so that "through . . . the encouragement of the Scriptures we might have hope."[5] Not to know those Scriptures is to deprive ourselves of confidence in God's faithful love.

Why Jesus?

"Jesus is the answer," crow billboards, bumper stickers, and even restroom walls. Occasionally one finds scrawled below it, "But what is the question?" It's a fair rejoinder. Jesus Christ has to have a context if he is to mean anything. And this was as true in the first century as it is today.

Jesus clearly did have a context in the first century—the revelation of the Scriptures that then existed, what we call the Old Testament. The disciples knew these Scriptures well, and when they finally understood how Jesus fulfilled them, their lives changed dramatically. They worshiped Jesus enthusiastically, they proclaimed him with fervor, they died willingly for him—and the world has never been the same.

What does Jesus mean to you? Why did he come? Why did he suffer and die—and then rise from the dead and ascend into heaven? What difference does the drama of Jesus' life and work make in your life today? These questions demand answers if Christianity is to come to life for us. And we cannot begin to answer them without knowing something about the setting in which Jesus lived, taught, and died.

The Old Testament anticipates Jesus, not simply by predicting events in his life, but also by showing us what we

5   Romans 15:4.

need him to do for us and why that need is so desperate. A wise suitor will do more than declare his love for the one he seeks to marry. He will convince her that she needs him. Our God has done this for us in the Old Testament. To be ignorant of those Scriptures is to be like the complacent husband, bored with his wife because he has never realized what life would be like without her.

Aged Simeon, well versed in the Old Testament, knew very well what life was like without the Messiah. For that reason, he had long been "waiting for the consolation of Israel." When he saw the infant Jesus in the temple, he took him in his arms, praised the Lord, and said he was ready to die, "for my eyes have seen your salvation."[6] Simeon's knowledge of the ancient Scriptures was deep, and therefore his joy in the Redeemer was strong. Should we not learn from him?

Questions for Discussion and Reflection

1. According to this chapter, what does a Christian believer miss by not knowing the Old Testament well?
   a. Can you think of other reasons why a Christian should know the Old Testament well?
2. What do Romans 15:4 and 2 Timothy 3:15 tell us about God's purpose for the Old Testament?
   a. In what ways is Christ at the center of this purpose?
3. How do we know that Genesis 3:15 is much more than a primitive explanation of the hatred that exists

6 Luke 2:25–32.

between women and snakes? Second Corinthians 11:3, 14–15 and Romans 16:20 will help.

4. Imagine yourself as Eve, hearing Genesis 3:15 for the first time, without the benefit of any further revelation.

   a. How would you feel?

   b. What questions would the promise raise in your mind?

   c. How might you identify the "seed" of the woman?

5. Imagine yourself as Eve, having just heard that Cain murdered Abel. How might you now identify the "seed" of the woman?

6. How is Paul's experience of God's grace like Eve's (see 1 Corinthians 15:8–10; 1 Timothy 1:12–14)?

   a. List and discuss similar experiences from both Scripture and life.

   b. Take some time to thank God for his mercy.

7. Martin Luther said that Genesis 3:15 "embraces and contains within itself everything noble and glorious that is to be found anywhere else in Scripture."

   a. What did he mean?

   b. Do you agree?

Chapter 2

An Unfolding Mystery

I love mysteries. It is great fun to curl up with a book by Dorothy Sayers or Ngaio Marsh, juggling the unfolding evidence in an effort to determine who the culprit is.

One of the many reasons why I love Old Testament history is that it is a grand mystery story. (Paul actually uses the word *mystery* to describe it.[1]) Its scope is cosmic. Its resolution is dramatic and wondrous. And it is full of little mysteries. The biblical story begins with the cryptic promise we discussed in chapter 1 (the first "clue") and unfolds in a series of promises, all rooted in and driven by the first, until all the promises finally fit together like pieces of a puzzle at the coming of the Messiah.

In Genesis 3:15, God promises Eve a seed. She must have wondered long over that promise. Who would this conquer-

---

1   See Ephesians 3:1–6. Although Paul's use of the term *mystery* is not precisely equivalent to ours, the notion of hidden truth gradually revealed is common to both uses of the word.

ing offspring be? When would he come? Would the "seed" be the entire human race, or a particular child, or a special group within the human race? After all, the word *seed* was often used collectively, and Eve was the mother of all people. But then God said, *"He* shall bruise the head of the Serpent," and that language suggests that her promised offspring would be a single individual.[2] Time passed, and Eve bore two sons. As she watched them grow into men with profoundly different spiritual orientations, she might well have begun to think of two humanities, one born of the promise and the other born of the Serpent.

Slow Beginnings

Ambiguities in the identity of the promised seed notwithstanding, God makes it clear in Genesis 3:15 that through that seed he will undo the mess we have brought upon ourselves. From that time on, the Scriptures give careful and hopeful scrutiny to Eve's posterity.

The search nearly fails at the outset. Cain murders his brother and in so doing seems to put the promise in jeopardy. With Abel, the godly son, dead, what hope is there for a renewed race? But God mercifully intervenes and gives to Adam and Eve another son, Seth, who carries the good seed forward. Once again, however, our hope falters. As generation follows generation, the human race disintegrates morally, until at the time of Noah the heart of man is "only

---

2 This language does not absolutely prove that one individual is in view, since Hebrew idiom often uses singular personal pronouns in a collective sense (see Isaiah 44:1–2, 21).

evil all the time." The seed of Satan seems to have utterly overwhelmed the seed of the woman.[3]

Indignant over human rebellion, God cleanses the earth with the mighty Flood and starts over. He establishes Noah as a second Adam, charging him to "increase in number and fill the earth," and promising with the sign of the rainbow never again to destroy the earth with a flood. But the influence of the Serpent persists. In just a few short generations, Noah's descendants conspire to build "a tower that reaches to the heavens . . . [to] make a name for [themselves]." God sees the project as a satanic assault on his authority and judges it by dividing the human race.[4]

What has become of God's promise to set enmity between the seed of the woman and the seed of the Serpent? The two seeds seem to be perpetually in cahoots. The godly seed seems to be, at best, a tiny group, barely visible within the mass of humanity.

A Hopeful Focusing

Our hope revives with Abraham, a descendant of Noah's son Shem. The Lord promises special blessing to Shem's family and begins to make good on that promise with Abraham:

> The LORD had said to Abram, "Leave your country, your people and your father's household and go to the land I will show you. I will make you into a great

---

3   Genesis 6:1–6 seems to depict men deliberately choosing to unite with the seed of Satan.
4   See Genesis 9:1, 12–16; 11:1–9.

nation and I will bless you; I will make your name great, and you will be a blessing. I will bless those who bless you, and whoever curses you I will curse; and all peoples on earth will be blessed through you."[5]

Genesis 3:15 echoes throughout this great promise. God takes the initiative, promising that he will act to bring blessing to Abraham. God calls Abraham away from his home and heritage, putting enmity between Abraham and the corrupted world around him. He promises to curse those who curse Abraham, bringing his judgment upon the seed of the Serpent in Abraham's name. And God promises universal blessing through Abraham's seed, making it clear that his intention in the ancient promise was to spare the human race through Eve's special descendant(s).

Having chosen Abraham to be the father of the promise, God narrows the focus even further. Of Abraham's sons, Ishmael and Isaac, he chooses Isaac. Of Isaac's sons, Jacob and Esau, God chooses Jacob.[6] And through his sons, Jacob becomes the great nation of Israel.

But the narrowing of the search for the seed of the woman continues. On his deathbed, Jacob pronounces a series of oracles regarding his sons, one of which especially draws our attention to the ancient promises:

> Judah, your brothers will praise you; your hand will be on the neck of your enemies; your father's sons

5 Genesis 12:1–3. Genesis 9:26 records the promise to Shem.
6 Genesis 25:12–18, 19–23; 26:2–4; 28:10–15.

will bow down to you. . . . The scepter will not depart from Judah, nor the ruler's staff from between his feet, until he comes to whom it belongs and the obedience of the nations is his.[7]

Judah will reign supreme, subduing his enemies (crushing the Serpent's head?) and receiving praise and obedience from his brothers. This arrangement will prevail until the coming one, whose reign will be universal, and who will himself most likely be of the tribe of Judah.[8]

A Long and Painful Wait

How distressing it must have been for the faithful Jew to ponder Jacob's great oracle during the cruel years in Egypt. Most of us have difficulty believing God's promises if he fails to fulfill them within a week. Imagine still waiting for God to come through on a promise made to your ancestors on the day the Mayflower sailed from Europe! That's how long the people of Moses' day had been waiting for the fulfillment of the promise given through Jacob. Many of us have difficulty believing that God loves us when a child is sick for a month.

---

7 Genesis 49:8–10.

8 The language of this oracle does not demand that the coming one be of the tribe of Judah, but it strongly suggests it. "If it were otherwise, [the coming one] would not have been alluded to in connection with Judah at all. [Such a] restriction of the promise to Judah . . . is the less legitimate, inasmuch as, in vv. 8–9, victory and dominion, without any limitation, are promised to Judah" (C. W. Hengstenberg, *The Christology of the Old Testament* [reprint, McLean, Va.: MacDonald Publishing Company, n.d.], 47).

Imagine trying to believe that your family is going to achieve international prominence when all three of your children have perished in an increasingly vicious slave state and your newborn and only grandson is about to die by government decree. Israelite families endured this in Egypt.[9]

The Lord's ways are not our ways, and with him a thousand years are as a day. He remembers promises that we have long forgotten or mistrusted. At the moment of Israel's greatest distress, the Lord intervenes, wonderfully sparing a little Hebrew boy and raising him up in Pharaoh's court to be a deliverer. Through Moses, God keeps the promise alive, liberating and establishing his people.[10] After testing them in the wilderness for forty years, God gives them the land that he promised to Abraham centuries earlier.

David: the Great Forerunner

The nationalism in Jacob's oracle takes shape in Canaan, where the monarchy emerges under King David. His predecessor, Saul, is a false start from the wrong tribe (Benjamin), yet he establishes the context in which a shepherd boy from the tribe of Judah can rise to prominence. David defeats the mighty Goliath, catching Saul's eye, and he is drawn into the royal circle, where he quickly becomes a favorite of the king. Unfortunately, he also becomes a favorite of the people, which turns Saul's love to murderous jealousy, forcing David to flee for his life into the wilderness.

---

9 See Exodus 1.

10 Exodus 2:1–10. Moses also kept the promises alive by committing them to writing for all to know and remember; see chapter 1.

14

After Saul's death, David gradually consolidates power and emerges as king over all of Israel's tribes.

The saga of David and Saul in 1 Samuel 8–31 is a marvelous story, full of love, loyalty, courage, despair, tragedy, intrigue, and triumph. It is also, at its deepest level, an unfolding in human history of Genesis 3:15. The falling out between the two men is not merely a human drama. A cosmic and supernatural war drives their differing attitudes toward God and toward each other, the darkness that falls upon Saul's heart (leading him eventually to mediums), the drive in Saul to see David dead, and David's loyal refusal to retaliate. Saul hates David because the Serpent, operating in the benighted king, knows David to be in some sense the descendant of Eve sent to crush his head.

In many ways, David fulfills the ancient promises. He is a godly man, at odds with the seed of the Serpent. He defeats God's enemies in battle. As Jacob predicted, this son of Judah receives the highest praises of the people ("Saul has slain his thousands and David his ten thousands!"). In keeping with the promise given to Abraham, he makes of Israel a nation to which the surrounding world looks for leadership. But David is a man of war, and the promises call for universal peace. David is also a sinner, and the promises call for a man of unfaltering righteousness, utterly at enmity with the Serpent.[11] And so when David proposes to

---

11 Genesis 49:10 promises a king out of Judah, and 1 Samuel 13:14 tells of David's suitability for that role ("a man after God's own heart"). But Genesis 49:10 also seems to call for a king of peace ("Shiloh" most likely comes from the Hebrew word meaning "rest"), and 2 Samuel 7:9 and 23:13–39 remind us that David was a man of war.

build a permanent house for the Lord, the court prophet, Nathan, says no:

> When your days are over and you rest with your fathers, I will raise up your offspring to succeed you, who will come from your own body, and I will establish his kingdom. He is the one who will build a house for my Name, and I will establish the throne of his kingdom forever. I will be his father, and he will be my son. When he does wrong, I will punish him with the rod of men. . . . But my love will never be taken away from him, as I took it away from Saul, whom I removed from before you. Your house and your kingdom will endure forever before me; your throne will be established forever.[12]

Not David, but his son, will set up the promised reign, and the reign will be eternal. David must have wondered who this son would be. Would it be one of his many children, or a descendant of one of his offspring?

Hindsight is twenty-twenty, and we know that Solomon fulfilled Nathan's words, at least in part, when he built the temple. But Solomon died and his kingdom quickly began to disintegrate, exhibiting little evidence of the flourishing and eternal "house" predicted by Nathan. So who is the son in view? In a pattern typical of prophecy, God says things that apply both to the immediate future (that is, to Solomon and the kings who succeed him) and to the distant future

12   2 Samuel 7:12–16.

(that is, to the Messiah).[13] Solomon will build the temple in Jerusalem. Solomon and subsequent kings will know the chastisement of foreign nations. But beyond them will come another, the eternal king, the ultimate son of David, the seed of the promise.

The wait is long and disheartening. Two hundred and fifty discouraging years after David, Isaiah rekindles our hope:

> The people walking in darkness have seen a great light; on those living in the land of the shadow of death a light has dawned. You have enlarged the nation and increased their joy; . . . For as in the day of Midian's defeat, you have shattered the yoke that burdens them, the bar across their shoulders, the rod of their oppressor. . . . For to us a child is born, to us a son is given; and the government will be on his shoulders. And he will be called Wonderful Counselor, Mighty God, Everlasting Father, Prince of Peace. Of the increase of his government and peace there will be no end. He will reign on David's throne and over his kingdom, establishing and upholding it with justice and righteousness from that time on and forever. The zeal of the LORD Almighty will accomplish this.[14]

---

13 This pattern is called prophetic foreshortening. The prophet sees two or more future events as one, just as an explorer might see two distant mountain ranges as one because of his inability to see the valley between them.

14 Isaiah 9:2–7.

Isaiah knew what God had promised Eve and the patriarchs and David. He also knew the frightful apostasy of so many of the kings since David's day. For all of these reasons, he saw that our hope must rest in an extraordinary child given to us by God himself, a child who would be mighty, tender, righteous, and divine. David's son would have to be God's son.

The Seed Preserved

For a thousand years, from the day God promised David a son to the day Gabriel spoke to Mary, God kept the line of David intact. He did this despite civil war, bloody political intrigue, deportation, and many generations of subjugation to foreign powers. Around 850 B.C., for example, Athaliah slaughtered all of David's descendants and declared herself ruler of Judah. One small prince, Joash by name, miraculously escaped her rampage and was hidden away in the temple for six years. When the prince reached the age of seven, Jehoiada the high priest revealed him to the people and reinstituted the legitimate monarchy.[15]

First Chronicles 1–10 has about as much appeal to the average Christian reader as a Moscow telephone directory does to the average American teenager. But all the names in these chapters matter in the light of the promises we have been discussing. They comprise a genealogy, meticulously recorded to remind us of God's faithful preservation of the seed of Abraham and, more particularly, of the seed of

15 2 Kings 11:1–16.

David's tribe, Judah. They remind us that God never forgot his promise to Eve.

A Striking Pattern

What did Sarah, Rebekah, and Rachel have in common? They were all barren, and yet they were all selected in God's providence to bear children of the promise. In each case, the Lord intervened dramatically to open the womb. He came to Sarah in her old age and gave her Isaac, despite her laughing unbelief (the boy's name means "laughter," a gentle rebuke from God). He gave Jacob and Esau to barren Rebekah, Isaac's wife. And he gave Joseph, and later Benjamin, to barren Rachel.

Other women cried out for children at critical moments in redemptive history. Manoah's wife longed for a child, was visited by an angel, and gave birth in time to Samson, the great champion over the Philistines. A short time later, Hannah begged the Lord to open her womb, and he heard her prayer, giving her the great prophet Samuel, who directed the critical years of Israel's fledgling monarchy.[16]

This pattern of events reminds us that the rescue of the world is the Lord's work from start to finish, that "salvation comes from the LORD." In Genesis 3:15, God teaches us to set our hopes upon a child. He then proceeds repeatedly to make the birth of that child humanly impossible, so that we might learn to ask with wonder and

16 See Genesis 18:9–15; 21:1–7; 25:21; 30:23; Judges 13:2–25; 1 Samuel 1:1–20.

hope the question he put to Sarah, "Is anything too hard for the LORD?"[17]

It should not surprise us that the child of our hopes should also come miraculously. God does what we cannot do, and in this case even beyond what we can imagine: "The virgin will be with child and will give birth to a son, and will call him Immanuel." When Mary asks Gabriel, "How will this be, since I am a virgin," Gabriel tells her that the Lord himself will overshadow her and she will bear a child by God's own "seed," as it were.[18] In this great and astounding act of God, the Serpent's doom is sealed. Now, finally, for the first and only time in human history, a son of Eve is also fully the Son of God. God finally makes the enmity between the woman and the Serpent complete and unbreachable. Only by such a child—and surely by such a child—can the supernatural enemy of God and man be annihilated.

From his place of exile, the aged apostle John saw a furious and immense red dragon threatening a woman of great splendor and beauty:

> The dragon stood in front of the woman who was about to give birth, so that he might devour her child the moment it was born. She gave birth to a son, a male child, who will rule all the nations with an iron scepter. And her child was snatched up to God and to his throne. . . . Then the dragon was enraged at the

---

17 Genesis 18:14. Jonah summarizes, "Salvation comes from the LORD" (2:9; cf. Psalm 3:8).

18 See Luke 1:34–38; Isaiah 7:14.

woman and went off to make war against the rest of her offspring—those who obey God's commandments and hold to the testimony of Jesus.[19]

John saw in a single vision the furious enmity that has dominated human history at its deepest level. The woman is Eve, Sarah, Mary, the church—all those who are the objects of God's gracious promise. The dragon is the beguiling Serpent, seething with hatred and bent on destroying God's plan for the world's redemption. Ever since God spoke in the Garden, Satan has feared and hated childbirth. The barrenness of Sarah, Rebekah, and Rachel, Athaliah's attempt to murder the royal line, the slaughter of the innocents in Bethlehem— all were his malevolent work, a desperate attempt to destroy the seed of promise, thereby averting the curse on himself.

The dragon mounted his final and most furious assault on Good Friday. At the cross, he humiliated and hoped to destroy the promised child. But that child was "caught up to God and to his throne," for death could not hold the one who in life had never aligned himself with the Serpent. Thwarted again and again through redemptive history, the Serpent was on Easter vanquished forever by the son of Eve. He can now only rage against us in a fury inspired by defeat and humiliation as he awaits his destruction.

The Mystery Solved

God solved the "mystery" of Genesis 3:15 when he sent his Son. We imagined earlier how Eve must have tried to

19 Revelation 12:4–5, 17.

identify the promised seed. Would it be the entire human race, or a particular child, or a group of her offspring? God's answer in Christ wondrously encompasses all three possibilities. The victorious offspring is, of course, preeminently a single child, our Lord Jesus Christ.

But Christ is not alone, for he is the Second Adam, the "everlasting Father" of a new race. God binds us to him so tightly that what is true of him becomes true of us, either now or in a guaranteed future (theologians call this "union with Christ").[20] This means, among many other wonderful things, that if he is the promised seed, then we who believe in him are also that seed. When Paul speaks of God "soon crush[ing] Satan under [our] feet," he has this very idea in mind.[21] We, through union with Jesus, fulfill the promise made to Eve.

Would the promised offspring be the whole human race or a group of people? Christ answers that question as well, drawing together under his wings a universal family, not in the sense that all people are saved, but in the sense that the saved come from every culture and walk of life.[22]

God gives us much more than a great mystery story in the search for Eve's offspring. He reminds us along the way that he is the God of miraculous mercy. He loves to rescue

---

20 The idea of our union with Christ appears in the frequently used New Testament phrases "in Christ," "through Christ," and "with Christ." Romans 5:12–21 and 1 Corinthians 15:12–28 discuss his role as the Second Adam.

21 Romans 16:20.

22 Galatians 3:28–29.

weak and rebellious people—people who, like us, are sold out to the Serpent and unable to help themselves. "Is anything impossible for God?" is always his question to us.

The Lord shows us something else. He reminds us that he can be trusted. He may speak mysteriously in Scripture. He may take ages to fulfill what he has promised to do. But he keeps his word. Dozens of prophets wrote the Bible, and they did so over more than ten centuries. The preoccupation with Eve's seed began at the dawn of human history and was passed down by oral tradition to the time of Moses, who committed it to writing. The promise remained on the hearts of biblical writers for well over a thousand years until the apostle John, in exile on Patmos, saw and described its happy fulfillment. Such unparalleled literary coherence, such beauty, and such rich fulfillment proclaim that behind the many authors of Scripture stands one Author—an Author who has given us a book that we can trust, an Author who keeps his promises.

Questions for Discussion and Reflection

1. At least five themes appear in the great promise of Genesis 3:15: (1) redemption is God's work ("I will put . . ."); (2) spiritual enmity will characterize human history ("I will put enmity . . ."); (3) redemption will be won by the woman's seed ("he shall bruise your head"); (4) the promised seed will suffer ("you shall bruise his heel"); (5) redemption will be universal ("her seed"). Trace these themes as they appear in each of the unfolding promises of redemptive history:

- to Abraham (Genesis 12:1–3)
- to Judah (Genesis 49:8–12)
- to David (2 Samuel 7:11–16)
- to Isaiah (Isaiah 9:2–7)
- to the "Son" (Psalm 2)
- as fulfilled in Christ (Hebrews 2:10–18)

2. We have seen in this chapter that we can identify the promised seed both as the Messiah and as the messianic people.

   a. Consider the messianic role of the Jewish people: In what ways have they brought blessing to the world through suffering? How have the Jews been a source of universal blessing (Luke 3:23; Romans 3:2; Philippians 3:5)?

   b. Are the Jews alone the promised seed (see Romans 10:9–13)?

   c. Are all the Jews the promised seed (see Romans 2:25–29)?

   d. What do we mean when we say that the human race is the promised seed (Revelation 7:9–10; 21:3; 22:2, 14–15)?

   e. On what basis can we say that believers are the promised seed (Romans 8:16–17; Galatians 3:28–29)?

3. The line of promise is full of unexpected characters. What makes each of the following people unlikely candidates for the messianic line?

   - Jacob (Genesis 27:18–29)
   - Tamar (Genesis 38)
   - Rahab (Joshua 2:1; see Matthew 1:5)

- Ruth (Ruth 1:4)
- Judah (Wouldn't one of Joseph's children make more sense, given his heroic and godly role?)

   a. Why did God choose such a line of people? (See Romans 9:10–13.)

4. Galatians 3:26–29 puts you, if you are a believer, in the messianic line, along with all the characters listed in question 3. How do you react to belonging to such a group?

   a. Spend some time thanking God for his grace toward you.

5. Believers are identified with the promised seed because of their union with Christ. His role and privileges become theirs. What practical difference does being "in Christ" have for

   - evangelism and spiritual warfare (Romans 16:20)?
   - service (Luke 9:23)?
   - growing in godliness (Romans 6:10–11)?
   - facing failure and discouragement (1 Corinthians 15:58)?

6. The God of the promises is the God of the impossible. Take fifteen minutes to list all the miraculous deliverances in Scripture that come to mind.

   a. From what has the Lord delivered you?

7. Reflect on the following "mystery" passages in the New Testament: Ephesians 1:9–10; 3:2–13; Colossians 1:25–27. What do they teach about

   - how long ago the mystery was planned?
   - the role of Jesus Christ in revealing the mystery?
   - the content of the mystery?

Chapter 3

CLOSE ENCOUNTERS

"If only God would do something tangible! Then I'd believe in him." I often hear this complaint. We are creatures who live in the world of the senses, and we long for God to meet us on our own turf.

He has. Biblical history reveals a God who continually penetrates the "real world." Not only did he create all things, but he walked with Adam, talked to Moses "face to face," thundered from Sinai, led his people as a pillar of fire, fed them manna, disciplined them with snakes, healed them, and lived in various "houses" built by them. And finally he took on human flesh.

Visits from the Son

We know that God came to us in the person of his Son. But few of us realize that the Old Testament appearances of God were also visits of the Son. Those visits were designed to whet our appetite for the Incarnation.

Whose back did Moses see at Sinai? With whom did Jacob wrestle? Who appeared to Abraham by the oaks of Mamre? The Scriptures say it was the Lord. But the Scriptures also say that "no one has ever seen God."[1] The apostle John addresses this problem by telling us that it was the second person of the Trinity. The Son (John also calls him "the Word") has always been active in the world, expressing God's power in creation and God's truth in a darkened world. His role from the beginning has been to make God tangible.[2]

Brief Encounters

Lovers cannot bear to be apart. Phone calls and long letters do not satisfy the longing to be together; they only intensify it. The Old Testament appearances of the eternal Son are like those phone calls and letters. They are temporary, incomplete, and distant, designed to awaken in us a longing for God's permanent, intimate, full, and gracious appearing in the Incarnation.[3]

The Lord appeared to the patriarchs on numerous occasions. He came to Abraham in his ninety-ninth year to renew his covenant promises. Later he dined with him under the oaks of Mamre and promised a child for Sarah within the year. He warned Isaac not to seek aid from Egypt during

---

1   John 1:18; see also Genesis 18; 32:22–32; Exodus 33:21–23.
2   See John 1:1–18. Although v. 18 ("No one has ever seen God, but [the Son] . . . has made him known") focuses on revelation after the Incarnation, it expresses the pattern that has always been followed (see vv. 3, 5, 9–10).
3   See John 1:14, 16–18; Hebrews 1:1–3.

a famine, guaranteeing instead his own protection and blessing. Some time later, God met Isaac in Beersheba and renewed the covenant promises. He appeared at least twice to Jacob, once as a nocturnal wrestler and a second time to renew the promises of the covenant.[4] He ministered tenderly to Hagar in the desert, called Moses from the burning bush, and received Joshua's worship on the eve of Jericho's fall.[5]

All of these appearances, though generally intimate and encouraging, were brief and rare. Abraham lived for decades between visitations. As far as we can tell, Isaac and Jacob each had only two such encounters.[6]

A Distant Nearness

On the day Israel left Egypt, these sporadic encounters gave way to something more permanent:

> By day the LORD went ahead of them in a pillar of cloud to guide them on their way and by night in a pillar of fire to give them light, so that they could travel by day or night. Neither the pillar of cloud by

4 Genesis 17:1–22; 18:1–15; 26:1–5, 23–24; 32:24–31 (note that Jacob treats the wrestler as divine); 35:9–13.

5 Genesis 16:7–13; Exodus 3; Joshua 5:13–6:2. These last three instances involve "the angel of the Lord," a figure whose title distinguishes him from the Lord, and yet who speaks and receives worship as the Lord. This ambiguity suggests the Trinity.

6 All these instances describe actual appearances of the Lord. Other visitations may have been visions (see Genesis 15) or words alone (see Genesis 22:11, 15). But even these visitations were few and far between.

day nor the pillar of fire by night left its place in front of the people.

In this form, the Lord protected and guided the Israelites until they entered the Promised Land. The cloud stood between them and the wrath of Egypt by the shores of the Red Sea. It covered Mount Sinai when Moses received the Law. It stood at the door of the Tent of Meeting whenever Moses chose to seek God's counsel. Then it settled permanently in the tabernacle upon its completion, rising only to lead the people forward on their journey.[7]

How comforting all this must have been to ancient believers. In the days of Abraham, Isaac, and Jacob, the Lord appeared only to a select few. But in the days of Moses, every man, woman, and child could see the Lord at any time, hovering over the tabernacle or standing before the Tent of Meeting. At the time of the patriarchs, the Lord appeared unpredictably. Now Moses had only to seek his presence at the Tent of Meeting and the Lord would "speak to [him] face to face, as a man speaks with his friend." The Lord was in the cloud, and the cloud never left.[8]

But there were problems. Not everyone had the access to God that Moses had, and very few people seemed to want it. When the Lord shook the earth at Sinai, the people begged Moses to do all the talking for them. The fire and cloud that had only recently delivered them from certain

---

7 Exodus 13:21–22; 14:19–20; 19:16; 33:9; 34:5; 40:36–38; and Numbers 10:11–12 document the watch-care of the pillar of cloud.

8 Exodus 13:21; 33:11; see also 33:9; 34:5.

death at the hands of Pharaoh now filled them with terror. And not even Moses' access to God was all that it could be. On the day of the tabernacle's completion, God's glory descended with such frightful brilliance that not even the great prophet could enter the Tent of Meeting.[9]

Israel's relationship to God in Moses' day was something like a marriage without affection. It had permanence without intimacy. The design of the tabernacle stressed this: God lived there, close to his people, and yet hardly anyone could ever go into his living room. To enter the Holy of Holies through the veil, except at the prescribed time and using the prescribed preparations, meant death. Those with permission to enter found there neither a lover nor a cordial host—nor even a monarch. They found an awesome presence, sometimes visible in a cloud, hovering over a man-sized, empty throne.[10]

We are not saying that the eternal Son was passive during this time. To the contrary, he gave himself dramatically and mercifully to meet Israel's needs. He sent the Israelites food in abundance, quail by night and manna by day, the latter without fail for forty years. He gave them water in the wilderness, at least three times miraculously. He delivered

---

9 Exodus 20:19 (see 19:16–20:21); 33:9–10; 40:33–35 (see also 1 Kings 8:10–11). Encountering the living and holy God undoes us (cf. Isaiah 6:1–5).

10 See Leviticus 16 (esp. v. 2). Exodus 26:31–33 describes the veil, and Exodus 25:10–22 the ark of the covenant. The latter was covered by the mercy seat, and formed the throne from which the invisible God spoke his commandments to Moses.

them from fierce enemies and the judgments brought on by their own hard-heartedness.[11] Yet despite all this activity, the Lord remained distant.

This pattern continued into the period of the Conquest. No longer visible as the guiding cloud, the Lord revealed himself even more dramatically as a mighty warrior:

> This is how you will know that the living God is among you and that he will certainly drive out before you the Canaanites. . . . See, the ark of the covenant of the Lord of all the earth will go into the Jordan ahead of you.[12]

With breathtaking speed and finality, the army of Israel, led into battle by the ark, conquered the cities of the Promised Land. Impregnable Jericho fell first, its mighty walls crumbling miraculously before the Lord. Then, one by one, the others followed until all the land lay subdued before them.

And yet the Lord remained distant. When he appeared to Joshua as "commander of the army of the LORD," the leader "fell facedown to the ground," undone by the glory. Thirty-six soldiers died tragically and an entire family suffered stoning at the Lord's command because Achan, the head of that family, disobeyed God. Years later, when Israel sought to use the ark magically to subdue the Philistines in battle, thousands of Hebrew foot soldiers perished and the

---

11   Exodus 16 (esp. v. 35); 15:22–25; 17:1–7; Numbers 20:2–13 (see 1 Corinthians 10:4); 21:4–9.
12   Joshua 3:10–11.

ark was taken. Later still, David's joyful march to Jerusalem ended abruptly when Uzzah reached out to steady the ark and was struck down by God on the spot.[13]

We expect intimacy and tenderness from one who lives with us continually, especially if he or she has promised to love us for life. To be without that intimacy, even when the person provides materially for us, is troubling and at times unbearable. Such was the problem with the pillar and the ark. God's constant nearness was tantalizing. It kept hinting at an intimate relationship that never materialized.

Words of Love

When I first met the woman I was eventually to marry, I sought as many opportunities as I could to be near her and do things for her. This was great fun, but it was not enough. It became obvious that all this activity needed interpretation. So, during the first summer of our acquaintance, I began to write her regularly. Our correspondence grew steadily in its depth and became the heart of the relationship that issued in marriage.

The eternal Son's wooing of us is like that. At the time of Moses and Joshua, he drew near to his people and did many wonderful things for them. But his presence and deeds needed interpretation if Israel was to understand them to her benefit. So the mighty Word became the communicating Word. Beginning with Moses, he inspired

---

13 Joshua 5:13–15; 7:1–26; 18:1 (see 21:43–45); 1 Samuel 4 documents Israel's ill-conceived efforts to use the ark, and 1 Chronicles 13:9–10 tells of Uzzah's sudden death.

prophet after prophet to sing to his people the warnings and promises of his love. Some prophets committed their "songs" to writing, thus creating our Old Testament. Others, in God's providence, did not.[14]

These words, both written and spoken, were as tangible a sign of God's love as the glorious pillar and the conquering ark. They were in fact a fuller sign, for they made clear and unchangeable the nature and terms of the relationship that he meant to establish with us. Without these words, God's actions (however kindly intended) would not have had any certain meaning. Israel's relationship to him would have foundered on the rocks of ambiguity. Try to imagine a friendship without communication, and you will see how empty the events of Moses' and Joshua's day, not to mention the history that followed, would have been without the Scriptures.

Departing Glory

The eternal Son made God's love tangible. He delivered Israel from Egypt, protected her in the wilderness, gave her

14 Moses wrote or compiled most of the first five books (called the Pentateuch). From Samuel's day on, "schools" of prophets were continually active in Israel, directing and encouraging the king. Geerhardus Vos explains why they did not begin writing until the middle of the eighth century B.C., as the kingdom declined: "The word of the earlier prophets, though a truly divine word, had been largely a transient word, intended for their own day and generation. But from this second crisis onward the word ever increasingly obtained reference to the new creation of the future, and consequently dealt with things in which future generations would have a share and supreme interest" (*Biblical Theology* [Grand Rapids: Eerdmans, 1948], 208).

the Promised Land, and made her a wealthy and powerful nation.[15] He also spoke to her clearly and earnestly by faithful prophets, drawing near through his word.[16]

Then he left. The fall of Jerusalem was more than the brutal subjugation of a city to Babylonian might. By it God declared that he had abandoned the city he had once called his own. Jeremiah understood this and wept bitterly over it:

> The Lord has rejected his altar and abandoned his sanctuary. He has handed over to the enemy the walls of her palaces; they have raised a shout in the house of the LORD as on the day of an appointed feast. . . . My splendor is gone and all that I had hoped from the LORD.

The Lord's word left with his presence. One hundred and fifty years before the fall of Jerusalem, Amos had predicted "a famine of hearing the words of the LORD." As years passed, God spoke less frequently and more stridently, until he virtually stopped speaking altogether. Writing on the eve of Jerusalem's fall, Ezekiel cried:

> Calamity upon calamity will come, and rumor upon rumor. They will try to get a vision from the prophet;

---

15 Ezekiel 16:1–14 portrays the Lord's care in the imagery of adoption and marital love.

16 "The word is very near you; it is in your mouth and in your heart so you may obey it" (Deuteronomy 30:14).

the teaching of the law by the priest will be lost, as will the counsel of the elders.[17]

A brief flurry of prophetic, apocalyptic, and historical Scripture attended Israel's return from exile (the revival that began with Haggai's call to rebuild the temple in 520 B.C. and concluded with the end of Nehemiah's labors in 433 B.C.),[18] but after that, silence reigned for over four hundred years.

The Word Became Flesh

With encouragement from Hosea, we can describe Israel's relationship to the Lord throughout the Old Testament as a young and struggling marriage.[19] But what a marriage! At first, the groom rarely shows himself. When he does appear, it is without warning and for brief visits only. Eventually he comes to live in the home of his wife, but remains austere and unapproachable. His words of love, at first full of warmth and promise, become less frequent and more heated, until they cease altogether. And then, with creditors and hoodlums at the door, he walks out on her.

Why was there such a marriage? One fitting answer is that the bride was a mess. The groom remained distant and even-

---

17 Ezekiel 7:26 (see Micah 3:6–7). Jeremiah's cries appear in Lamentations 2:7; 3:18, and Amos's in Amos 8:11.

18 Also set in this period are the books of Zechariah (whose night visions were concurrent with the prophecies of Haggai), Esther (during the reign of Ahasueras, sometime after 486 B.C.), Malachi (full of warnings just prior to Ezra's restoration, probably about 460 B.C.), and Ezra (who probably began his reforms in Jerusalem in 458).

19 Hosea 2:19–20; see Ezekiel 16:3–14.

tually withdrew altogether because his betrothed continually broke her vows.[20] A deeper reason is that the groom wanted to make clear to his people, and through them to the world, that what we really needed was the Incarnation and the blessings that flow from it. The Incarnation closes the gap between our experience and God's. It means that we now have a husband who fully understands us because he has walked in our shoes. Talking clouds don't experience birth, pain, temptation, and death, but Christ was "tempted in every way, just as we are—yet was without sin." It also means that our husband will continue to understand us, for the Incarnation was not for a brief span (as were the appearances to the patriarchs), but lasts forever: "Jesus . . . has a permanent priesthood. . . . He always lives to intercede for [us]."[21] And it means that we have a husband who reveals God perfectly to us. His self-portrait is flawless because he is the eternal Word. It is understandable because he is human.[22]

Christmas paved the way to Good Friday. Without the Crucifixion, there might well be a sympathetic groom, but there would be no bride:

> Christ loved the church and gave himself up for her to make her holy . . . and to present her to himself as a radiant church, without stain or wrinkle or any other blemish, but holy and blameless.[23]

20 Hosea vividly documents Israel's spiritual adultery. See also Ezekiel 16:15–48.

21 Hebrews 7:22, 24–25 (see also 13:8); Hebrews 2:17–18, 4:15, and 5:7–8 document the fulness with which Jesus shares our humanity.

22 John 1:14; see Colossians 1:15, 19; Hebrews 1:1–3.

23 Ephesians 5:25–27.

The groom endured a long, distant, and rocky relationship to convince us that nothing short of his own sacrificial death would make the marriage work. The Cross alone makes us fit to be his bride.

The Cross led to Easter and Pentecost, and with the gift of the Spirit came the gift of intimacy that had so long eluded God's people. The terrifying glory that had formerly settled behind the heavy curtain in the temple came to settle in human hearts made habitable by the Cross. God's people became God's temple. The groom came on Pentecost to live in us forever. And he came not to the select few, as formerly, but to "all flesh."[24]

God has done something tangible, hasn't he? He has wooed us patiently through a long, troubled history. He has become one of us, living, suffering, and dying as a human being. And he has done all this so that we might know him intimately, as a bride knows her husband. One day, and it may be soon, he will return for us. At that moment, we will be transformed into a bride of unimaginable beauty. And then we will dine with him at the marriage feast of the Lamb, our marriage feast.[25]

Questions for Discussion and Reflection

1. Read John 1:1–18 and answer the following questions:

   a. Why does John describe Christ as "the Word"?

   b. How long has the Word been active?

---

24 First Peter 2:4–10 describes us as the holy temple built by Christ. See also Acts 2:17 (quoting Joel 2:28).

25 Revelation 19:7.

   c. What have been the Word's functions (vv. 1–4)?

   d. How, according to verses 10–11, has the Word generally been received?

   e. If John 1:18a is true, how do we explain Genesis 12:7, Genesis 17:1, Genesis 35:9, Exodus 3:3–6, and Numbers 12:6–8?

   f. Isaiah 6:1–5 and John 4:24 (see also 1 Kings 8:27 and Isaiah 40:12–31) give at least two reasons why seeing God is a problem for us. What are they?

2. The angel of the Lord appears numerous times in Old Testament history (Genesis 16:7–13; 22:11–12, 15–18; 24:7, 40; 31:11; 48:16; Exodus 3:1–6; 23:20–21; Joshua 5:13–6:2).

   a. What various functions does the angel serve in these passages?

   b. Look carefully at the angel's dealings with Hagar (Genesis 16:7–13). Is the angel God or a representative of God (compare vv. 10 and 13 with v. 11)?

   c. Note the tenderness of the angel—to a non-Jew. What great promise does this remind us of (see Genesis 12:3 and Acts 15:6–11)?

   d. Look carefully at Jacob's wrestling bout (Genesis 32:22–32). Did he struggle with God or with an angel (compare Genesis 28:15–16 and Hosea 12:4 with Genesis 32:28, 30 and 35:9)?

   e. How does John 1:1 help us explain the identity of the angel who appeared to both Jacob and Hagar?

3. Compare Exodus 3:13–14 with John 8:58–59. According to Jesus, who appeared to Moses in the burning bush and who subsequently led Israel out of

Egypt and into the Promised Land? What additional insight does Paul give us in 1 Corinthians 10:1–4?

4. Imagine growing up in Moses' time, living with the constant presence of the pillar of cloud and fire. In what ways would that presence have been an assurance to you, and in what ways a terror? The following passages will help: Exodus 13:21–22; 14:10–20 (esp. vv. 19–20); 20:19 (see 19:16–20:20); 33:9–11; 40:33–35.

5. In Exodus 23:20–21, God says, in effect, "My name is in the angel."

   a. What relationship exists between God and his name (Deuteronomy 12:5, 11; Psalms 48:10; 83:17–18; 86:11; Isaiah 42:8)?

   b. Compare this relationship to the one that Jesus says exists between the Father and the Son (John 5:19–23; 10:38; 14:10; 17:21; cf. Colossians 2:9).

6. Read Ezekiel 16:1–43, Hosea 1–3, and Ephesians 5:25–33.

   a. What imagery does God use to describe his relationship to Israel? What does this reveal about his attitude and feelings toward Israel? Toward you?

   b. What does God do for Israel, and how does she respond?

   c. What explanation do the passages give for the Lord's abandonment of Israel? What hope do they give for a renewed relationship (see Hosea 2:16–23 especially)?

   d. Why, according to Ephesians 5, can the marriage work?

   e. What does being God's bride mean to you?

Chapter 4

FINDING CHRIST IN
OLD TESTAMENT CHARACTERS

Fascinating people fill the pages of the Old Testament. I cannot think of any other single volume in literature that contains such a wealth of characters. Brooding Cain murders his unsuspecting brother and then defies God with those troubling words, "Am I my brother's keeper?" Courageous and beautiful Queen Esther, an orphan and exile in Persia, risks her life to rescue her people: "If I perish, I perish." There is Uriah, loyal soldier to the end, who won't go home to be with his wife—even at David's invitation. And there is King David, adulterous and desperate to keep that adultery secret, who appalls us by contriving Uriah's death in battle. Jacob connives, robbing his brother and lying to his ailing father. Jezebel murders, bending King Ahab to her will, slaughtering God's prophets, and dying as violently as she lived. Young Solomon chooses wisely, seeking wisdom over fame, but later in life drifts into the idolatry of his many foreign wives. Jonah (our favorite reluctant evangelist) runs from his task and pouts when he eventually succeeds. Full of the courage of faith, Elijah stands alone against the prophets of Baal.[1] The list goes on and on.

Much has been written and said about these and other Old Testament characters. Sadly, a great deal has tended to be moralistic: i.e., "David slew his Goliath; now you go out and slay yours!" Can you see the problem with this approach? When people present Old Testament characters primarily as examples (either good or bad), they make of the Old Testament much less than it was intended to be. They make it indistinguishable from any good literature designed to instruct us on better living.

The Old Testament Scriptures claim not only to inform, but also to transform: "The law of the LORD is perfect, *converting* the soul; the testimony of the LORD is sure, *making wise* the simple." Paul makes the same point in the New Testament:

> The Holy Scriptures [what we call the Old Testament] . . . are able to make you wise for salvation through faith which is in Christ Jesus. All Scripture is given by inspiration of God . . . for instruction in righteousness, that the man of God may be complete, thoroughly equipped for every good work.[2]

---

1 We find these characters and stories in Genesis 4:8–9; 25:29–34; 27:1–29; 2 Samuel 11:11–25; 1 Kings 3:3–9; 11:1–13; 18:4, 11–40; 21:25–26; Esther 4:16; Jonah.

2 Psalm 19:7 KJV; 2 Tim. 3:15–17 NKJV.

The Scriptures (including the accounts of the diverse characters we find there) were given to change us, and they do so by pointing us not to ourselves but to Jesus.

A Key Question

Our study of Old Testament characters should cultivate in us a love for Jesus, who said, "Apart from me you can do nothing," and who alone is "our wisdom, our righteousness and sanctification and redemption."[3] A good way to cultivate this love is to keep asking, "How does this character propel me to the Lord Jesus Christ, so that in him I may grow in godliness and hope?"

Numerous answers present themselves:

1. This person's godly example drives me to the Lord Jesus for power to be like him (Daniel in the lion's den).
2. His experience of divine wrath drives me to the Lord in holy fear (Moses barred from Canaan).
3. His experience of God's electing love and faithfulness, despite his sin and frailty, drives me to praise the Lord Jesus for his grace and compassion (Jacob the conniver is blessed).
4. Her experience of deliverance against great odds drives me to a deeper trust that I too will be saved and vindicated by the Lord Jesus' hand (Esther among the Persians).
5. His innocent suffering drives me to look for One who will make things right again and give meaning to the pain (Job: see Psalm 73).

3   John 15:5; 1 Corinthians 1:30 RSV.

6. His transformation from unbelief to strong faith fills me with wonder at the kindness, wisdom, and power of the Spirit of Christ (Jacob changes from manipulation in his youth to deep trust in his old age).

7. His imperfect performance in a leadership role drives me to adore Christ (by contrast) and appreciate him more fully as my only truly sufficient deliverer, friend, teacher, and Lord (Samson, the deliverer, is vindictive and promiscuous).

8. His righteous suffering in a leadership role prefigures the suffering of Christ and leads me to adore him with fuller understanding (David driven from Jerusalem by Absalom or fleeing from Saul in the wilderness).

9. Their faithful performance in a leadership role fires my imagination with a picture of the character and work of the true Messiah and whets my appetite for his return (Elijah's and Elisha's compassionate, bold, and powerful prophetic ministries).

Two Levels

Old Testament characters point to Jesus Christ at two levels. Answers 1 through 6 above reflect the first level, where we see them as fellow believers on the pilgrimage of faith, the "cloud of witnesses" whose faith in the coming Messiah challenges and encourages our own faith.[4] Answers 7 through 9 reflect the second level, where we see the characters as symbols, or types, of the One who is to come.

4   See Hebrews 11:1–12:3, esp. 12:1.

Fellow Pilgrims

Hebrews 11:1–12:2 introduces us to the first level, elaborating on the faith of Old Testament characters and concluding,

> Therefore, since we are surrounded by such a great cloud of witnesses, let us throw off everything that hinders and the sin that so easily entangles, and let us run with perseverance the race marked out for us. Let us fix our eyes on Jesus, the author and perfecter of our faith, who for the joy set before him endured the cross, scorning its shame, and sat down at the right hand of the throne of God.

Who are the "cloud of witnesses" and what are they doing? Perhaps they are people like Moses and Abraham, watching from the stands and cheering us on as we run the race of faith. Perhaps they are the same people witnessing to us by means of the race they have already run. Perhaps both views are intended: the Old Testament saints show us how to live by faith, and they watch us as we actively trust the One who was their hope.

In either case, whether they are watching us or we are watching them, these saints of old motivate us to "fix our eyes on Jesus, the author and perfecter of our faith." Their faith points us to Jesus, and it does so in at least three ways: he is the object of their faith, he is the perfect model of their imperfect faith, and he is the builder of their faith.

First, Christ was the object of their faith. Consider Moses, for example:

> By faith Moses, when he had grown up, refused to be known as the son of Pharaoh's daughter. He chose to be mistreated along with the people of God rather than to enjoy the pleasures of sin for a short time. He regarded disgrace for the sake of Christ as of greater value than the treasures of Egypt, because he was looking ahead to his reward.[5]

As we look to Jesus, we know that we are not running the race by ourselves. We are surrounded by people like Moses, who have run it before us. Although they did not know the Messiah's name, they demonstrated a faith in him that teaches and encourages us.

Secondly, Old Testament saints model (imperfectly) the life of faith that comes to perfect expression in Jesus, the "man of faith par excellence."[6] In other words, we learn from their example something of what it would mean for Jesus to put his life fully into God's hands. Their faithfulness anticipates the perfect faithfulness of the great Savior, who is their (and our) substitute, not only in his death, but also in the way he lived. When, for example, Abraham offered up Isaac, confident that God would somehow fulfill his promise of a great nation, he was imperfectly mirroring the faith of Jesus, "who for the joy set before him endured the cross, scorning its shame." When Moses forsook the pleasures of Pharaoh's court to "share ill-treatment with the people of God," he was imperfectly model-

---

5 Hebrews 11:24–26.

6 Philip Edgcumbe Hughes, *A Commentary on the Epistle to the Hebrews* (Grand Rapids: Eerdmans, 1977), 522.

ing the one who "did not count equality with God a thing to be grasped, but emptied himself, taking the form of a servant."[7]

A map points us in the right direction, but directions alone cannot bring us home. Few of our country's settlers would have made the trek west with nothing more than a compass and a map; they needed an experienced guide—someone who knew the trail well and who possessed the fortitude to bring them through to the end. Jesus is such a guide. We call him the great "pioneer" of faith because he blazed the trail of faith to the very end. We might say that Abraham got us to West Virginia, but that Jesus took us through to the West Coast.

Perfect Model, Certain Hope

It is Jesus' perfection as the pioneer or model of faith that makes him the absolutely trustworthy object of faith. David might well inspire us, but he could never save us, since his faith was imperfect. But David's son fulfilled all righteousness in our place, and is able therefore to bring us home. His faithfulness makes our faith count.

To say that Jesus is both the object and the model of faith is to discover that he fulfills the old covenant from both sides. As Edmund Clowney points out, he is both the Lord of the covenant and the Servant of the covenant.[8] On the

---

7 Philippians 2:6–7 RSV; Hebrews 11:17–22, 11:23–29, 12:2 describe, respectively, the faith of Abraham, Moses, and Jesus.

8 "Christ the Lord is confessed as God the Son in the New Testament. He is also revealed as the Servant. He comes to do the will of His Father." Edmund P. Clowney, *The Unfolding Mystery* (Phillipsburg, N.J.: Presbyterian and Reformed, 1988), 201.

one hand, we look to him as the one who sets the terms, who makes and keeps the promises, and who administers both the blessings and the curses of the covenant. On the other hand, we look to him as the one who keeps the terms, who trusts the promises, who obeys the commands, and who endures the curses and in the end receives the blessings—all in our place.

Did Moses know the human name of Christ? No. Did Abraham know in detail how the heavenly country would be won for him? No. But their limited knowledge did not keep them from looking to the same Savior in whom we trust. Jesus Christ has always been the hope of his people, whether they have known his name or not. Abel, Enoch, Noah, Sarah, Joseph, Rahab, Gideon, and so many more all looked to Jesus Christ, for they "all died in faith," looking to the promises of God, the promises whose final "yes" is in Jesus Christ.[9]

The Author of Faith

The faith of Old Testament characters points to Jesus in a third way. It shows Christ at work as the author of faith, planting faith in the barren soil of human hearts and causing it to grow despite all sorts of opposition. The Spirit of Christ, who leads us to understand Jesus, was active in Old Testament times, pursuing his loved ones and enabling them to look away from their circumstances to his provision.[10] Abraham began his pilgrimage because the Re-

---

9 2 Corinthians 1:20; Hebrews 11:13 RSV.

10 See John 14:15–17, 25–26; 16:5–15. Peter reminds us that it was "the Spirit of Christ" who inspired the prophets (1 Peter 1:10). A likely rendering of Jude 5 refers to "Jesus, who saved a people out of the land of Egypt."

deemer came to him, telling him to leave his home and journey to a land he did not know. The Redeemer loved dis-
honest and greedy Jacob, pursuing him until he became a
man of faith, reconciled to the brother whom he had
cheated, and committed to the promises of God.[11] The
Spirit anointed David king while he was still a shepherd and
propelled him into the life that made him a "man after
God's own heart." Esther learned to throw herself on the
Lord's mercy because her natural beauty and Haman's hatred of the Jews compelled her in God's providence to do so.
All of these saints learned to look to God's promises because
the Lord himself enabled and obliged them to do so. Scripture sets forth their lives as objects of Christ's searching and
transforming love, reminding us that "he who began a good
work in [us] will bring it to completion at the day of Jesus
Christ."[12]

The Second Level

On a fateful October morning during my senior year in
high school, I declared my faith at a school assembly—my
first public declaration in a hostile setting. That moment
ushered me in a very small way into the company of figures
like Polycarp, Luther, and Corrie Ten Boom, who stood
their ground at great cost. It also gave life to the story of
David and Goliath: I tasted something of David's lonely

---

11 Although living comfortably in Egypt at the end of his life, Jacob
    commanded his sons to bury him in the land of promise. See Gene-
    sis 49:29–32.
12 Philippians 1:6 RSV.

faith against great odds (a classmate, upon hearing my talk, told me that it was the worst thing he had ever heard), of David's marvelous and life-changing deliverance (God met me in a remarkable way the moment I stepped up to the platform), and I was encouraged. Thanks to David, my struggle to live out my faith found a stirring and biblical context. I was not alone.

Old Testament characters do this for us. But many of them, including David, help us at another level as well. Not only their faith, but also their role, points us to Christ. Prophets like Jeremiah, Elijah, and Isaiah foreshadow the ministry and character of the Word made flesh. Priests like Aaron anticipate the day when all of God's people will come with a clear conscience into his presence. And leaders like Samson, David, Josiah, and Nehemiah prefigure a King who will deliver his people from all their oppressors and rule them with justice and love. None of these is everything he should be. In fact, some of them fail miserably in their tasks. The inadequacies and failures, as we shall see later, point us toward Christ by setting up a frustrated longing that only he can satisfy. They whet our appetites for him.

A Rich Interweaving

The interweaving of these two levels beautifies and enriches Scripture. Take, for example, David's battle with Goliath. At one level, David fights as a fellow believer, our brother in Christ. He has known God's deliverance in the past, and he loves his deliverer. Goliath's mockery of God makes David so angry that he is ready, even eager, to put himself on the line. His courageous words stir our hearts:

You come against me with sword and spear and javelin, but I come against you in the name of the LORD Almighty, the God of the armies of Israel, whom you have defied. This day the LORD will hand you over to me, and I'll strike you down and cut off your head . . . and the whole world will know that there is a God in Israel. All those gathered here will know that it is not by sword or spear that the LORD saves; for the battle is the LORD's and he will give all of you into our hands.[13]

The Lord honors David's faith, guides the stone, and vindicates him, not only before the pagan enemies, but also before the frightened Israelites.

But there is another level, a deeper and more cosmic level. God has secretly anointed David king, filled him with his Spirit, and called him to represent God's kingdom against the forces of darkness. David's victory is much more than another exciting story of the underdog who comes out on top. Triumphing through David, God gives us a sneak preview of the ultimate triumph of David's greater son. David's hidden kingship, his zeal for God's glory, his human weakness, and his unexpected victory all foreshadow the coming Cross and Resurrection.

How do we apply the story of David and Goliath to our lives? We do so by rejoicing in the victory of Christ prefigured so vividly here, and trusting our Redeemer, as David did, to cast the works of Satan from our lives. We can do so, not because we are strong, or because the works of Satan are

---

13   1 Samuel 17:45–47.

few and weak, but because "he who is in [us] is greater than he who is in the world."[14] We are anointed by the same Spirit who possessed David.

Questions for Discussion and Reflection

1. What do we mean by a "moralistic" approach to the study of Old Testament characters, and what is wrong with it in the light of John 15:5, 1 Corinthians 1:30, and the "I will put . . ." principle found in Genesis 3:15?

2. What do Romans 15:4 and 2 Timothy 3:14–15 tell us about the intention of the Old Testament Scriptures, and what guidelines do they give for how we are to benefit from the study of Old Testament characters?

3. Read quickly through Hebrews 11:1–12:2. What is the common thread running through the lives of all the Old Testament saints, and what insight does this give us on how to study their lives in a Christ-centered way?

4. What are the two different levels at which Old Testament characters point us to Christ?

5. Consider Esther. How does her *faith* direct us to the Messiah? How about her *role?*

14   1 John 4:4.

Chapter 5

JOSEPH LOOKS TO CHRIST: A CASE STUDY

Troubles almost 'whelm the soul;
Griefs like billows o'er me roll;
Tempters seek to lure astray;
Storms obscure the light of day:
But in Christ I can be bold,
I've an anchor that shall hold.
And it holds, my anchor holds;
Blow your wildest, then, O gale,
On my bark so small and frail:
By his grace I shall not fail,
For my anchor holds, my anchor holds.[1]

Could Joseph have sung the words of this old hymn?
Could he have sung about being bold in the Messiah and
about being secure in him through the storms of life? How

---

1 "My Anchor Holds," by W. C. Martin.

we answer these questions reveals much about our understanding of what we discussed in the previous chapter. The answer that does justice to our Lord's own teaching about the Old Testament is a resounding yes!

We must grant, of course, that Joseph's understanding of the Christ was not as full as our own, but Hebrews 11 teaches that Joseph made it through his arduous life by looking to him, just as we do. If this were not so—if his way of "getting through" was not essentially the same as ours is now—then we could learn nothing of lasting value from him. He would be just another example of a man who "pulled himself up by his own bootstraps," the sort of man the Bible says has never existed.

Joseph's Story

Most of us know the story of Joseph (you can find it beginning in Genesis 37). He is the great-grandson of Abraham, the father of Israel. He grows up as the favorite of Jacob's twelve sons, both because he is "the son of [Jacob's] old age" and because he is the only son of Jacob's beloved wife Rachel.[2] Alone among his brothers, he receives a special robe from his father and seems to be sent by him to spy on his siblings. On one occasion he brings back a bad report on them to Jacob. Their father's attitude arouses a strong animosity among Joseph's brothers toward Joseph.

Making matters worse are Joseph's two dreams, the first of which depicts his brothers bowing down to him, and the

---

2 Genesis 37:3 RSV. Benjamin, Rachel's other boy, is still too young to occupy Jacob's attention.

second of which includes his parents doing the same thing. Rather unwisely, it would seem, the young man tells the dreams to his family, sealing his own doom in the process.

Some time later, Jacob sends him out to see how his brothers are doing (another spy mission?) and they nearly kill him. Deflected from their original plan by the compassion of the oldest brother, Reuben, they sell Joseph to some slave traders who take him to Egypt, where he becomes an important servant in the household of Potiphar, one of Pharaoh's officials. But when Potiphar's wife fails in her attempt to seduce Joseph, she turns against him and charges him with attempted rape. Joseph's infuriated master confines him to prison, where Joseph again prospers and becomes the means by which Pharaoh's chief butler and chief baker learn the meaning of some troubling dreams. The butler, who is shortly released, promises to put in a good word for Joseph, but he forgets to do so, leaving the young man languishing in jail for another two years.

The Hebrew's ability to interpret dreams eventually gets back to Pharaoh at a time when the king has endured some particularly trying ones. Joseph interprets Pharaoh's nightmares correctly and is promoted on the spot to his right hand, from which place of authority he conducts a brilliant famine relief program. Thanks to Joseph's diligence and skill, Egypt and the nations around her escape the horrifying devastation of a seven-year famine. Most notably, Joseph's own family is saved. In fulfillment of his dream, they come and bow before him in search of bread. He meets their need, reveals himself to them, and eventually moves them to Egypt, where they live and prosper for many years.

Joseph's story is an amazing tale of intrigue, hardship, and eventual vindication, ranking for sheer adventure with the works of Robert Louis Stevenson. More deeply, it is a story about the Redeemer. At one level, it documents a man's growing faith in the Messiah; at another level, it vividly pictures the work of the Messiah.

Level 1: Joseph's Growing Faith

We have probably all heard meditations on young Joseph's attitudes at home, his temptations in Potiphar's household, and his hopes and trials in prison. In actual fact, the biblical story tells us next to nothing about these things. Not until he is reunited with his brothers do we get a good look into Joseph's heart.

Why this silence? First, because the story is more about the Lord than it is about Joseph. Joseph's role as God's deliverer is more basic to the story than his faith, as we shall see later. Second, the silence reminds us that Christ creates and nurtures faith. He comes to us long before we come to him, using the circumstances of life to produce faith in him. Repeatedly, as the story unfolds, we note God's activity: "and the Lord was with Joseph," "and the Lord gave Joseph favor," "and the Lord caused. . . ." When, after more than two years in prison, Joseph is brought before Pharaoh to explain his dream, he declares with the humility born of the Lord's initiating love, "I cannot do it, . . . but God will give Pharaoh the answer he desires."[3]

Christ produces such faith in Joseph that, when his fa-

3 Genesis 41:16.

ther dies and his brothers come to him in fear of retribution, he is able to look back upon their cruelty and say,

> Don't be afraid. Am I in the place of God? You intended to harm me, but God intended it for good to accomplish what is now being done, the saving of many lives. So then, don't be afraid. I will provide for you and your children.[4]

Joseph has learned to see through circumstances and beyond them to the loving purposes of God. And he has learned to trust God's purposes so fully that he is able freely to forgive those who hurt him. In other words, God's promises—not human circumstances—have come to govern his life.

Joseph's confidence in the promises never fails. The latter years of his life are very comfortable years. He enjoys prosperity in Goshen and lives to see his family grow to the third generation. And yet he never forgets that God's promises rule history and must therefore be his only hope and delight. As he nears death, Joseph directs his family's gaze toward Canaan, securing from them a vow that his bones will be delivered there at the time of God's choosing. Although he does not know what we know about Christ, Joseph does know that life's hopes must be centered in God's plans and nothing else. So he looks to the promises that God gave to Abraham, promises whose full meaning we have come to see in Christ. He looks, in other words, to Christ.

---

4 Genesis 50:19–21.

Level 2: Joseph Foreshadows the Redeemer

There is a rich and striking parallel between Joseph's life and Jesus' life. Both men are sons of Abraham who are raised up to deliver their own people from death and in the process to bring blessing to the world. Both suffer great hardship at the hands of their own brethren. Both set their "family's" spiritual growth above their own needs. Both are falsely accused and punished for crimes they have not committed. Both are ultimately exalted to positions of great authority following their suffering—Joseph to Pharaoh's right hand and Jesus to "the right hand of the Majesty on high."[5]

This is no mistake. God gives us Joseph's story as a foretaste of his plan to rescue the world through the suffering of his Son. And he gives us also a glimpse of the experience of Jesus as we contemplate that of Joseph.

Consider, for example, the episode with Potiphar's wife and its aftermath. She accuses Joseph of the very crime he refused to commit ("How then could I do such a wicked thing and sin against God?"),[6] rewarding his righteousness with shame and imprisonment. How could this possibly be fair? Where was the God in whose name Joseph had driven off the woman's entreaties? Joseph's suffering is a picture of Christ's suffering. His faithfulness to God in the midst of injustice is a picture of Christ's faithfulness in similar circumstances.

Joseph's suffering prefigures Christ's most vividly when it is self-imposed. Consider Joseph's mystifying reception of his brothers when they come to him for help. How strange it is

---

5   Hebrews 1:3 RSV; see Genesis 41:37–40.

6   Genesis 39:9.

that he should at first conceal his identity: what better moment for self-disclosure than the moment when his brothers are on their knees before him, fulfilling his earlier dream!

Stranger still, he puts them through all sorts of difficulty. He calls them spies, throws them into jail for three days, suddenly releases them, binds Simeon before their eyes, and sends them back—without Simeon—to Canaan, warning them that if they return without Benjamin, they will die. He then fills their sacks with grain, returns their money without telling them, gives them provision for their return, and sees them off. When, after a long delay, the brothers come again to Egypt, this time with Benjamin, Joseph wines and dines them in his own palace and sends them happily home to their father, their sacks full of grain. Once again he secretly returns their silver and, going one step further this time, plants his personal cup in Benjamin's sack. Joseph's steward confronts the brothers on the road and they return in terror to Egypt, caught red-handed with stolen goods. Finally, with a cry that echoes through the palace, Joseph reveals himself.

Why this delay? And why all the cat and mouse? We know from Joseph's final outburst, as well as from an earlier one that he barely manages to conceal, that Joseph longs for reunion.[7] Even if he still resents his brothers, his longing to see his aging father must be overpowering.[8]

---

7 At the moment of the unveiling, he falls weeping upon their necks and kisses them, urging them not to be distressed or angry with themselves (Genesis 45:4–5,14–15). See also Genesis 42:23–24.

8 His first words to them are, "I am Joseph; is my father still alive?" (Genesis 45:3 RSV).

Love is the answer. His desire for reunion takes second place to his family's healing. And so he waits and manipulates circumstances to bring about the conviction of sin and the repentance that his brothers so desperately need. Their initial confinement leads to confession: "Surely we are being punished because of our brother."[9]

Overhearing these words spoken in his mother tongue, Joseph struggles to hide his emotions, but he still keeps silent. The greatest test is yet to come. To see if his brothers have really changed, he re-creates the original family scenario, this time with Rachel's other boy, Jacob's newly favored son. So Joseph binds up Simeon and waits for the arrival of Benjamin. When at long last Benjamin comes down to Egypt, Joseph works to stir up the old jealousy. Like Jacob of old, he lavishes his attention on Rachel's son, serving him fives times as much food as he serves the other brothers. Eventually he sends them on their way, but not without first planting his private cup secretly in Benjamin's sack, thus giving his brothers a strong incentive to betray the favored brother.

The scene unfolds dramatically shortly after the brothers' departure. Accused of stealing the cup, they protest their innocence vigorously and rashly, promising death to the culprit and servitude to themselves. Then to their horror they discover the cup with Benjamin.[10] Both at this point

---

9 Genesis 42:21. Reuben adds, "Did I not tell you not to sin against the lad? But you would not listen. So now there comes a reckoning for his blood" (v. 22 RSV).

10 Genesis 44:9–12.

and later in Joseph's own presence, the brothers are given complete freedom to abandon their little brother, but they refuse. Rather, they make public confession through Judah:

> What can we say to my lord? . . . What can we say? How can we prove our innocence? God has uncovered your servants' guilt. We are now my lord's slaves—we ourselves and the one who was found to have the cup.[11]

What a remarkable admission! They do not begrudge this miscarriage of justice because they know they are guilty of something much worse. What remarkable solidarity! If Benjamin is to be a slave of Pharaoh, they are too. God has indeed found them out.

But what triggers Joseph's self-disclosure is something greater still. Judah takes him aside and pleads with him, "Now then, please let your servant remain here as my lord's slave in place of the boy."[12] Like his great descendant Jesus, Judah offers his life in exchange for his brother's.

A hateful family was brought by Christ to heartfelt confession of its crime, a guilty family was forgiven by Christ and given the chance to try things over again—all through the loving patience of Christ's servant, Joseph. This is what we see in this strange series of interactions. Such love was costly to Joseph. He had to lay aside his right to be vindicated at the earliest possible moment. He had to put his longing for

---

11 Genesis 44:16.
12 Genesis 44:33.

reunion on hold. He had to risk never seeing his aging father again. Such self-effacing love reminds us of Jesus:

> Who, being in very nature God, did not consider equality with God something to be grasped, but made himself nothing, taking the very nature of a servant, being made in human likeness.[13]

Joseph: a Life from Which to Learn

The New Testament tells us that there is "one mediator between God and men, the man Christ Jesus."[14] He is able to "go between" (the meaning of *mediate*) because he is the God who has become man. He has faced the trials we face, as a fellow human being, having been tempted in every way, just as we have been, yet without sinning.[15] In Joseph's humiliation and exaltation, in his struggle to be faithful in the midst of extreme hardship, God gives us a vivid picture of the Messiah. Brought through deep waters to be the deliverer of his people, Joseph teaches us to expect a Messiah who, like him, will learn obedience through the things that he suffers.[16]

Joseph's anguish in suffering unjustly enables us to glimpse something of Christ's inner pain on the cross. Joseph's long wait for God to work his way in his brothers gives us insight into how Christ must have felt and how he must continue to feel as he painstakingly and tenderly works his way into our stubborn

---

13 Philippians 2:6–7.
14 1 Timothy 2:5.
15 Hebrews 4:15.
16 Hebrews 5:8.

hearts. And Joseph's joy at the healing and deliverance of his family points to the joy of the Resurrection, when the Messiah would see the result of his suffering and be satisfied.[17]

The challenge of Joseph's life is plain. Do we live by our Lord's promises or by our circumstances? When life becomes unmanageable—as it did so many times for Joseph—do we despair? Or do we press on obediently in what we know we must do, trusting that the Lord will vindicate us in his own way, according to his own timetable? When life is comfortable, do we grow cold to our Lord's priorities and plans? Or can we say, like Paul, "Forgetting what is behind and straining toward what is ahead, I press on toward the goal to win the prize for which God has called me heavenward in Christ Jesus"?[18]

The comfort of Joseph's life is also plain. Where did Joseph's godliness come from? Did he muster up the strength to "put a good face on things" in Potiphar's household and in jail? Did he teach himself compassion during a week of devotionals? Did he, after a few months of hard study, master the art of "seeing things God's way"? No. Joseph was a trophy of God's grace, patiently and tenderly molded by the Spirit of Christ through many long and difficult years. Joseph was taught by Christ to be like Christ, and so are we.

Questions for Discussion and Reflection

1. Look carefully at Genesis 39:1–2, 21–23.
   a. According to these verses, who is the principal actor in the story, the Lord or Joseph?

---

17   Isaiah 53:11.

18   Philippians 3:13–14.

b. What important lesson does this teach about how faith grows through trial?

2. Try to imagine what questions must have plagued Joseph when he was
   - thrown into a pit by his brothers.
   - taken in chains to Egypt.
   - thrown into prison for a crime he had faithfully refused to commit, and for which he was consequently framed.
   - left to languish for two more years because the butler forgot to speak up for him.

   a. What similar situations have you experienced?
   b. How did you respond to them?

3. Joseph's faith:
   a. Note how Joseph's growing faith came to expression in word and deed, according to the following passages:
      - Genesis 39:7–12
      - Genesis 41:16
      - Genesis 41:51–52
      - Genesis 45:5–8
      - Genesis 50:19–21
      - Genesis 50:22–25

   b. In what ways did Joseph's growing faith and faithfulness foreshadow Christ?
   c. How do his faith and faithfulness challenge you?

4. Joseph's role:
   a. How is Joseph's role like Christ's
      - in benefits to God's people?
      - in blessings to the world?

- with regard to personal suffering and glory?

b. How is Joseph's role different from Christ's
- in relation to the nature and degree of suffering each experienced?
- in relation to the scope and type of deliverance each man accomplished?
- in relation to the extent of each man's exaltation?

5. How does the life of Joseph propel you to the Lord Jesus Christ, so that in him you may grow in godliness and hope? Try to answer as fully and specifically as you can.

Chapter 6

Take My Yoke upon You

"My eight-year-old simply will not worship God with us. She just mumbles and grumps all through the service. What can I do?"

"But the Bridges are such godly people—and they only had one child. Why did their little girl have to die?"

"Our sex life is the pits. What can we do to make it better?"

"The new supervisor may be a hard worker, but he is misery to work for. He never has an encouraging word—hardly any words at all. What should I say to him, if anything?"

"Pastor Edwards has the troubling habit of visiting a number of single women in their homes in the evening. What should I do about this?"

"No one at work seems to like me. What am I doing wrong?"

"Bill had his heart set on getting that degree, and now he has failed his comprehensives for the second time. What do I tell him?"

"Ellen is a godly woman, and she clearly loves me. But should I marry her?"

All of these questions call for wisdom, the skill of living before God in the real world, of putting "godliness into working clothes."[1] And God has graciously given us that wisdom in his Word. Although the wisdom of the Lord may be found throughout the Scriptures, much of it appears in Job, Proverbs, Ecclesiastes, and the Song of Solomon.

Two Types of Wisdom

We can distinguish two different kinds of wisdom, didactic and reflective.[2] The first kind promises blessing for righteous living and warns of judgment for disobedience. Didactic wisdom fills the book of Proverbs especially. The person who fears the Lord, who lives conscientiously before him in the details of life, knows life in its fullness. Long life, riches, peace, food, authority, property, good friends, a joyous marriage, and a blessed posterity are all that person's inheritance.[3] "Happy is the man who listens to me," cries wisdom, "for he who finds me finds life and obtains favor from the LORD." The fool, by contrast, enjoys none of these benefits. For his refusal to heed instruction he receives bondage, poverty, loneliness, calamity, anguish, and death. Throughout Proverbs we hear the wise man saying, "He who is steadfast in righteousness will live, but he who pursues evil will die."[4]

---

1 Derek Kidner, *The Proverbs: An Introduction and Commentary* (Downers Grove, Ill.: InterVarsity Press, 1964), 35.

2 I am indebted to Dr. Bruce Waltke for this helpful distinction.

3 Proverbs 5:18–19; 10:3, 4, 27; 12:24, 21; 17:17; 18:22, 24; 20:7.

4 Proverbs 11:19 RSV; see Proverbs 1:24–32; 6:9–11, 23–29; 7:21–27; 8:34–35 RSV; 12:24.

What does it mean to be "steadfast in righteousness"? It means fundamentally to trust the Lord fully in every sphere of life:

> Trust in the LORD with all your heart and lean not on your own understanding; in all your ways acknowledge him, and he will make your paths straight. Do not be wise in your own eyes; fear the LORD and shun evil.[5]

We are to bring all our ways under his scrutiny, deeply confident that he knows better how to live than we do. Flowing from this wellspring of trust will be the marks of wisdom: teachability, marital faithfulness, gracious speech, generosity, hard work, honesty, and loyalty in friendship. The wise child learns gladly and humbly from his parents, knowing that such submission leads to the knowledge of God. The wise man bows to God's discipline, confident that "the LORD disciplines those he loves, as a father the son he delights in." The trusting husband rejoices in the wife of his youth, regardless of circumstances, knowing that the Lord has favored him with what is good. The wise woman's words will be like those of her Lord, "a fountain of life" to those who hear.[6] The godly man "gives freely" to the poor, knowing that God identifies with the needy and will enrich him for his generosity. The wise woman works hard because she

---

5 Proverbs 3:5–7.

6 Proverbs 1:8–9 (see also 2:1–5); 3:11–12; 5:18; 10:11; 13:14; 18:22 (see also the Song of Solomon, which models with great beauty and detail a wise man's devoted love for his beloved).

knows that the Lord will reward her with authority. The wise businessman shuns dishonesty in the marketplace, knowing his all-seeing Master abhors "diverse weights" and "false scales." The godly person is a good friend, even when it is costly, for this is pleasing to God.

Do you want life to run smoothly? Do you want prosperity, joy, meaning, and peace? Then take the wisdom of God to heart. It will be "a fair garland for your head" and lovely "pendants for your neck."[7] This is the promise of didactic wisdom.

Reflective Wisdom

Wait a minute, you say. Life isn't quite so simple. It may be generally true that those who live rightly live well. But I know plenty of decent folks (even believers) who are depressed, sick, and confused. What about that pastor's six-year-old who was abducted, molested, and killed? And what about that mudslide that wiped out a whole city? And how do we explain terrorists who never get brought to justice and corrupt politicians who stay in office?

These are questions of reflective wisdom, questions that life continually throws at us, and questions that the Bible itself asks. If Proverbs and the Song of Solomon contain the precepts of didactic wisdom, Job and Ecclesiastes rivet our attention on the problems of reflective wisdom. They look long and hard at life itself and raise the questions that at times seem to destroy the very heart of didactic wisdom.

7   Proverbs 1:9 RSV; see 11:24 (also 14:31); 12:24; 17:17; 20:10, 23 RSV.

Take Job, for example. Job was a good man. In fact, he was a deeply righteous man, "blameless and upright, one who feared God, and turned away from evil."[8] So commanding was Job's integrity that princes "laid their hand on their mouth" in his presence, nobles hushed, aged men rose, and young men withdrew. His wisdom drew ardent hearers:

> Men listened to me, and waited, and kept silence for my counsel. . . . They waited for me as for the rain; and they opened their mouths as for the spring rain.

The poor and needy knew his tender and aggressive care. The oppressor feared his righteous anger. Job never failed to hear with justice the concerns of his servants, he never defrauded his wife, he never "rejoiced at the ruin" of an enemy, he never even misused the land that God had given him.[9]

And yet Job suffered. In a brief span of time he lost his children, his possessions, and his health. Worse, he lost the respect of friends and the comfort of their company and esteem:

> I have become a laughingstock to my friends. . . . He has alienated my brothers from me; my acquaintances are completely estranged from me. . . . My kinsmen have gone away; my friends have forgotten me. . . . I summon my servant, but he does not answer.

---

8 Job 1:1 RSV.

9 See Job 29–31 for a detailed and moving account of Job's righteousness and tragic suffering.

Worse still, he lost the love and respect of his wife. Worst of all, God seemed to be set against him: "He would crush me with a storm and multiply my wounds for no reason." Repeatedly Job besought the Lord for an audience, begging him to explain how he could crush the righteous man and let the scoundrel go free. Apart from the comfortless judgments of his friends, he heard nothing:

> But if I go to the east, he is not there; if I go to the
> west, I do not find him. When he is at work in the
> north, I do not see him; when he turns to the south,
> I catch no glimpse of him.

Have you ever wished fervently that you had never been born? Job did. He cursed the day of his birth, calling down "darkness and deep shadow" upon it. "Why did I not perish at birth, and die as I came from the womb?" Life often brings such words to our lips.[10]

If Job reflects on the problem of suffering, Ecclesiastes ponders the problems brought on by prosperity. The Preacher has lived "the good life." He speaks as the mouthpiece of Solomon, the King of Israel's golden age, who denied himself nothing of God's great blessings. Whatever he desired he got—whether it was great learning and ability, or varied pleasures ranging from wine and sex to music, architecture,

---

10 Job 12:1–5 and 19:13–16 describe his loss of prestige. Job 2:9 and
19:17 document his wife's attitude. Job 9:17–20; 21:1–26; 23:8–9;
23:1–4; 13:3; 13:22–24; 24:12 describe God's silence and apparent antagonism. Job laments his birth in Job 3.

and horticulture, or strenuous, productive work. Yet "the good life" proved then as it does today to be strangely empty:

> "Meaningless! Meaningless!" says the Teacher. "Utterly meaningless! Everything is meaningless." What does man gain from all his labor at which he toils under the sun? . . . All of them are meaningless, a chasing after the wind.

Only fools and snapping puppies chase after the wind, for it cannot be held. Were it catchable, it would cease to be wind the moment we snared it. Meaning in life is like the wind, says the Teacher, and toiling to give life meaning is like chasing the wind.[11]

One warm, spring afternoon in my fourteenth year, while I was daydreaming about the coming summer, a disturbing thought came to mind: "Next year at this time I will once again be looking forward to the summer. And the next year. And the year after that." I suddenly realized that I was in the midst of a cycle that would repeat itself pointlessly throughout my life until I died. In my own words, I began to sing the sad song of the Preacher:

> The sun rises and the sun sets, and hurries back to where it rises. . . . All things are wearisome, more than one can say.[12]

---

11 See Ecclesiastes 2:10. Ecclesiastes 1:12–2:26 documents life's varied pursuits, and 1:2–3, 14 begins the repeated cries of vanity.

12 Ecclesiastes 1:5, 8.

Why are our efforts, even our efforts to live wisely before God, pointless? Because of death. When all is said and done, I am no better off than the wife beater next door or the deadbeat on skid row. In fact, I am no better off than my pet retriever:

> Man's fate is like that of the animals; the same fate awaits them both: As one dies, so dies the other.

Why work hard when the fruit of our labor may at any moment be stripped from us?

> A man may do his work with wisdom, knowledge and skill, and then he must leave all he owns to someone who has not worked for it.[13]

Life itself (let alone death) makes my efforts to be wise and diligent seem pointless. I may live to see that for which I have worked very hard suddenly become someone else's possession. Tyranny, disease, or a single unfortunate business venture can strip me of God's blessings. The righteous man "perishes in his righteousness," while the wicked man "prolongs his life in his evil-doing." Fools achieve political power while princes labor as slaves. The swift don't win races, the strong don't win battles, and the wise and intelligent go hungry. Not wisdom, but "time and chance" seem to rule.[14]

13 Ecclesiastes 2:21. Ecclesiastes 1:6, 8; 2:17–26; 3:19; and 9:2 itemize the futility brought on by death.
14 Ecclesiastes 9:11; Ecclesiastes 3:6; 4:1–3; 5:13–14; 6:1–6; 7:15 RSV; and 10:6–7 underscore the futility of life.

So much for the precepts of didactic wisdom! If Proverbs gives us the broad terms of the contract, Job and Ecclesiastes give us the fine print. And the fine print seems to void the heart of the document.

Jesus Christ: Our Wisdom

How does the Wisdom Literature show Jesus Christ to us? It forces two problems upon us that only Jesus can solve. The first is the theological problem we have been discussing. Proverbs says, "He who pursues righteousness and kindness will find life and honor." But Job says, "I am not at ease, nor am I quiet; I have no rest; but trouble comes." Proverbs says, "The hand of the diligent will rule." But the Teacher says, "The race is not to the swift."[15] Which is it going to be, moral principle or hard reality? Job learns that God holds the answer. But he must wait for Christ to unveil and extend it.

Jesus intensifies the problem by embodying it. He was the wisest man who ever lived. His speech was full of grace and power. He taught the way of love, and he practiced perfectly what he preached. Most significantly, he feared the Lord with all his heart, living in obedience even to the point of death. So pleasing was his life that the Father proclaimed from heaven, "This is my beloved Son, with whom I am well pleased."[16] No man before or since has received such praise.

Yet Jesus suffered the curses of the Wisdom Literature. He lived in poverty and died as a criminal in the prime of

---

15   Ecclesiastes 9:11; compare Proverbs 12:24; see also Job 3:20, 26; Proverbs 21:21 (all RSV).

16   Matthew 3:17; 17:5 (RSV) and parallels.

life, betrayed and abandoned by his closest associates. For his goodness he received hatred, mockery, and a crown of thorns. Worst of all by far, he was rejected by the God whom he had lived to serve.[17]

Jesus' life and death intensified the problems inherent in the Wisdom Literature. But the Resurrection resolved them. On Easter, the Father not only vindicated his Son, but also vindicated all of the promises of didactic wisdom. And he did so far beyond what the ancient teachers of wisdom could have imagined. The One who suffered untimely death has received eternal life in an incorruptible body. The One who died rejected and alone has received not just the honor of his friends, but the worship of the world and the angels. The One who lived in poverty "with no place to lay his head" has inherited not just a home, but the whole earth. The One whom God rejected receives from his Father the authority to judge all things.[18]

The resurrection of Jesus Christ lifts our eyes above the horizon of this world. It enables us to see with greater clarity what ancient wisdom, whose vision was confined to life "under the sun" (an often-used phrase in Ecclesiastes) struggled to see. Didactic wisdom shines forth as wondrously true in God's deliverance of his Son.

The Personal Problem

Why be wise? Why should I be sexually pure, asks the teenager, when TV and the movies tell me that all my friends

---

17 "My God, my God, why have you forsaken me?" (Psalm 22:1, quoted by Christ on the cross).

18 See 1 Corinthians 15:20, 35–57; Philippians 2:9–11; Hebrews 1:2.

are sleeping around and enjoying it? Why should I take that stand at work, asks the anxious young executive, when it may cost me my job? Why should I keep trying to love my husband, asks the frustrated wife, when he worships his career, ignores the kids, and treats me like a slave? Why even try to stop drinking, cries the despairing alcoholic, when every effort I've already made has failed?

These questions underscore the practical difficulty we have with the Wisdom Literature. It is one thing to know the way of wisdom. It is another thing to choose it.[19] Where do the motivation and ability to fear the Lord come from? I have often found the right path both easy and sensible. Equally as often, I have found it pointless, boring, and even impossible.

Take speech, for example. Proverbs gives us much sound advice about speaking,[20] but we continue to be destructive and divisive despite what we know. James puts the sad truth succinctly:

> The tongue also is a fire, a world of evil among the parts of the body. It corrupts the whole person, sets the whole course of his life on fire, and is itself set on fire by hell. . . . No man can tame the tongue. It is a

---

19 Notice how earnestly the father pleads with his young son in the first nine chapters of Proverbs. Such persuasion would be unnecessary if choosing wisdom were natural to us.

20 "Death and life are in the power of the tongue" (Proverbs 18:21 RSV). Cf. 10:11, 20–21, 31–32; 12:13–14, 17–19, 22–23, 25; 13:2, 3, 17; 15:1–2, 4; 20:19, 20, 25. These are only a sampling.

restless evil, full of deadly poison. With the tongue we praise our Lord and Father, and with it we curse men, who have been made in God's likeness.

My tongue is unruly, and it reveals a heart that is unruly, deeply resistant to the wisdom of God. What I need is a teacher of the heart, one who will subdue me inwardly.[21]

Jesus Christ is that teacher. He has all the skill necessary. After all, he grew up in the "real world," facing what we face, and learned how to subdue heart and speech to his Father. Consider the final hours of Jesus' life. Falsely accused, deserted by his friends, spit upon, and brutally beaten, Jesus was led forth to a humiliating and frightful death amidst the jeers of the very people whom he had come to redeem. Jesus had every "right" to be bitter. And yet his words were "a fountain of life." He prayed for his tormentors, answering violence with intercession. He commended his grieving mother to the care of the apostle John. And he promised life to the repentant thief who had earlier mocked him.[22]

Would you hire someone to coach you in tennis who has never played the game—or who has never played it successfully? Of course not. Jesus alone has successfully "played the game" of life. When he says, "Take my yoke upon you, and learn from me; for I am gentle and lowly in heart, and you

---

21 James 3:6–9. Matthew 12:34 reminds us that our words arise from our hearts, and Isaiah 30:20–21 anticipates the day when the divine Teacher will change our hearts.

22 Mark 15:34, Luke 23:43, and John 19:26–27 document Jesus' speech at the cross. See Proverbs 10:11; Hebrews 4:15.

will find rest for your souls," he is offering to be our "Coach." He is promising to lead us gently forward into the way of wisdom.[23]

How does he do it? By working from the inside out. Jesus is the perfect coach, not only because he knows the game perfectly, but also because he lives within us. The tycoon in *Heaven Can Wait*[24] can win the Super Bowl because the mind and spirit of the dead quarterback indwell him. I can walk today in the way of wisdom because the Spirit of Christ has entered my heart.

It's Worth the Effort

Jesus' resurrection proves that, however things may look, it is always smart to be wise. What seemed a tragic and pointless death turned out to be the key to life. Easter reminds us that God's ways are not our ways, that our seemingly pointless sufferings are not really pointless. God works in them, weaving from them a tapestry of glory. Easter also reminds us that God sees our struggles to live faithfully before him and rewards them. Jesus "endured the cross, despising the shame" because of "the joy that was set before him." We can too.[25]

---

23 Matthew 11:29 RSV. The yoke was a metaphor for wisdom in Jesus' day (see Ecclesiasticus 51:26).

24 In this film, the heavenly bureaucracy inadvertently removes a star quarterback from earth before his time. The film chronicles the effort to get him back into a body so that he can play in the Super Bowl.

25 Hebrews 12:2 RSV. Isaiah 55:8–9 reminds us that God's ways are not our ways, and Romans 8:18 (RSV) reminds us that "the sufferings of this present time are not worth comparing with the glory that is to be revealed to us."

Questions for Discussion and Reflection

1. Compare the following groups of wisdom verses:
   - Proverbs 2:1–5 and Ecclesiastes 1:12–18
   - Proverbs 11:8, 24; 14:31; 20:7; 21:13, 21 and Job 29–31
   - Proverbs 12:11, 24 and Ecclesiastes 5:10; 9:11
   - Proverbs 13:22 and Job 1:13–19; Ecclesiastes 6:1–2

   a. Identify the topics in each coupled group of verses.

   b. Distinguish between didactic and reflective wisdom in each coupled group of verses.

   c. Try to reconcile the two types of wisdom in each coupled group.

2. When Paul calls Jesus "wisdom from God" (1 Corinthians 1:30), he means among other things that Christ perfectly demonstrated God's wisdom in his life. How did Jesus "put flesh on" the following passages?
   - Proverbs 1:8 (see Luke 2:48–51)
   - Proverbs 3:5–6 (see Matthew 4:1–11; 26:39)
   - Proverbs 3:11–12 (see Hebrews 5:8–9)
   - Proverbs 10:11; 15:4; 18:21 (see Mark 4:39; 5:8, 15, 34, 41; 15:34; Luke 5:20; 23:43; John 15:3; 19:26–27)
   - Proverbs 11:24; 14:31; 21:13 (see Luke 7:18–23)
   - Proverbs 12:24, 27 (see Luke 2:49; 9:51–53)
   - Proverbs 14:27 (see Acts 2:24; John 4:34)
   - Proverbs 17:9; 27:6 (see Matthew 16:23; John 13:38; 21:15–19)

- Proverbs 17:17 (see John 15:13)
- Proverbs 18:24 (see John 14:16–18)
- Song of Solomon 8:6–7 (see Ezekiel 16:3–14 and Ephesians 5:25–33)

3. How does Jesus' resurrection resolve the theological problem inherent in the Wisdom Literature?

4. We have seen that Jesus Christ is our perfect wisdom "Coach" for two reasons: he knows the "game" of life, and he lives within us. How and why does this truth, elaborated in the following passages, motivate you to fear the Lord more fully?
   - John 14:15–18; 16:12–15
   - Hebrews 2:10–18
   - Hebrews 4:14–16
   - Hebrews 5:7–10
   - Hebrews 12:1–11

5. Jesus' resurrection proves that God rewards those who fear him, thereby motivating us to hang in there when the going gets rough. How do we keep the idea of rewards from undermining the message that we are "saved by grace through faith"?

Chapter 7

SONGS OF THE MESSIAH

Christians read the Psalms more than they read any other Old Testament book. And this makes sense, for no other book in the Bible gives such rich and beautiful expression to the ups and downs of the spiritual life. When I am depressed, it is immensely comforting to read, "Why art thou cast down, O my soul? and why art thou disquieted in me?" When I need to get "up" for worship, it helps to read, "Bless the LORD, O my soul: and all that is within me, bless his holy name."[1] When my heart is alive with praise, Psalm 145 and others like it add fuel to the fires of devotion. When I need a refreshing meditation on God's continual presence and intimate knowledge of me, I turn to Psalm 139.

The Psalms teach us how to see God's hand in nature. They teach us how to be honest about our sin. They teach us where to set the hopes of our hearts. They motivate us

---

1   Psalms 103:1 KJV; 42:5 KJV.

to heartfelt praise. They comfort us when we are depressed. They reassure us when others hurt us without cause. They remind us of God's faithfulness and deep deliverance. They promise his just and glorious reign on earth. Some psalms lend themselves to quiet contemplation, while others demand a thousand tongues and a brass choir. Some call forth tears of remorse, while others call forth cries of jubilation.[2]

The diversity and beauty of the book of Psalms feed us richly and have driven the life of devotion in God's people for three thousand years. Sadly, though, there is a dimension to the Psalms that we often miss. Reading them for their direct application to our own experience, we often fail to see their focus on the Messiah, the Lord to whom they are ultimately addressed. Many of the Psalms are messianic songs. Some are songs about the Messiah, and some are songs by the Messiah.

Songs About the Messiah

Many psalms focus our attention on the king of Israel. Certain psalms (21, 45) extol the king for his faith, beauty, majesty, and might. Others (20, 72) call for God's blessing

---

2   Psalms 8 and 104 rejoice in nature; 32 and 51 carry us into heartfelt repentance; 27, 73, and 84 focus our joy and hope on the Lord; 103 and 116 call forth our praise in the contemplation of the Lord's many mercies; 23 and 42 comfort us in depression; 17 and 26 offer reassurance when we are hurt by enemies; 40, 69, and 105 remind us of God's faithfulness and deliverance; 2 and 96 cast our gaze forward to the day of the Lord's universal reign; 121 and 131 draw us into quiet contemplation; 95 and 148 cry out in jubilation.

upon the king. Still others (2, 110) see him as the conqueror of the nations, enthroned by God's own power.[3]

These psalms (designated "royal psalms") envision a king so glorious in his might and so universal in his reign that they simply must be prophetic:

> [The king] asked you for life, and you gave it to him—length of days, for ever and ever. . . .
>
> You are the most excellent of men and your lips have been anointed with grace, since God has blessed you forever. . . . Your throne, O God, will last for ever and ever. . . . I will perpetuate your memory through all generations; therefore the nations will praise you for ever and ever. . . .
>
> He will rule from sea to sea. . . . All kings will bow down to him. . . . For he will deliver the needy who cry out, the afflicted who have no one to help. . . . May his name endure forever; may it continue as long as the sun. All nations will be blessed through him, and they will call him blessed.[4]

Such language goes beyond even the hyperbole that one might expect from a court poet seeking to declare his devotion to a local monarch. It envisions the coronation and reign of a man who is more than a man, a "man after God's own heart," whose rule will be without end. This vision is not

---

3 Other royal psalms include 60 and 144 (where the king cries out to the Lord for help) and 10 (where the king makes a vow of fealty to God).

4 Psalms 21:4; 45:2, 6, 17; 72:8, 11, 12, 17.

new to the Psalms, for it is already present in God's promises to Abraham, to Moses, and to David.[5]

Psalm 110 (together with Psalm 2) vividly proclaims the Messiah. Peter cites its opening verse at the climax of his stirring Pentecost sermon to explain the meaning of Jesus' death and resurrection. The psalm reads:

> The LORD says to my Lord: "Sit at my right hand until I make your enemies a footstool for your feet." The Lord will extend his mighty scepter from Zion; you will rule in the midst of your enemies. Your troops will be willing on your day of battle. Arrayed in holy majesty, from the womb of the dawn you will receive the dew of your youth. The LORD has sworn and will not change his mind: "You are a priest forever, in the order of Melchizedek." The Lord is at your right hand; he will crush kings on the day of his wrath. He will judge the nations, heaping up the dead and crushing the rulers of the whole earth. He will drink from a brook beside the way; therefore he will lift up his head.

David knew that God would one day enthrone a man far greater than himself (he calls him "my Lord"). This man would possess all authority and power at the Lord's "right hand." His glory would draw a host of eager volunteers, and

---

5 Genesis 12:1–3 promises that Abraham's offspring will be a blessing to the nations; Deuteronomy 17:14–20 promises Israel an ideal king; 2 Samuel 7:16 promises David an everlasting royal line.

his might would annihilate his foes. He would conquer and reign in such harmony with God ("the LORD") that they would be at each other's right hand (compare verse 1 with verse 5).

How can a human king, a son of David, be greater than David, the "man after God's own heart"?[6] How can one man bring all of God's enemies to their knees? How can a man confer glory upon God by calling him to battle at his right hand? When will this extraordinary man be crowned? Such questions arise out of this psalm. They find their answer in the drama of Jesus Christ, "descended from David according to the flesh and designated Son of God in power according to the Spirit of holiness by his resurrection from the dead."[7] Peter understood this and preached it vigorously on Pentecost:

> God has raised this Jesus to life, and we are all witnesses of the fact. Exalted to the right hand of God, he has received from the Father the promised Holy Spirit and has poured out what you now see and hear. For David did not ascend to heaven, and yet he said, "The Lord said to my Lord: 'Sit at my right hand until I make your enemies a footstool for your feet.'" Therefore let all Israel be assured of this: God has made this Jesus, whom you crucified, both Lord and Christ.[8]

---

6 In Mark 12:35–37, Jesus asks this very question about Psalm 110 while teaching in the temple, alluding in the process to his own messiahship.

7 Romans 1:3–4 RSV.

8 Acts 2:32–36.

Songs by the Messiah

The New Testament uses many psalms in an intriguing way: the words and experiences of David are put into the mouth and life of Jesus. "I will open my mouth in parables" describes Jesus' teaching method. He cleanses the temple, inviting the wrath of his enemies, because "zeal for [God's] house will consume [him]." Jesus predicts his sufferings and those of his disciples with David's words: "They hated me without a cause." As his passion draws near, Jesus describes his heart's turmoil in the language of Psalm 6: "Now is my soul troubled. And what shall I say? 'Father, save me from this hour'?" Three of Jesus' "seven last words" derive from the Psalms: "My God, my God, why have you forsaken me," "I thirst," and "Into your hands I commit my spirit."[9] John calls our attention to Psalm 22 when the soldiers divide Jesus' garments. Matthew structures the heart of his passion narrative around the suffering depicted in Psalms 22, 38, 69, and 109.[10]

Jesus' vindication, not simply his suffering, finds expression in the Psalms. Peter interprets the Resurrection by recalling Psalm 16: "You will not abandon me to the grave, nor will you let your Holy One see decay." Paul describes Gentile evangelism and conversion as the work of the exalted Christ singing Psalm 18:

9   Matthew 13:35 (see Psalm 78:2); John 2:16–17 (see Psalm 69:9); John 15:25 RSV (see Psalms 35:19; 69:4); John 12:27 RSV (see Psalm 6:3–4); Matthew 27:46 (see Psalm 22:1); John 19:28 RSV (see Psalm 69:21); Luke 23:46 (see Psalm 31:5).

10   John 19:24 (Psalm 22:18); Matthew 27:32–56.

For I tell you that Christ has become a servant of the Jews on behalf of God's truth . . . so that the Gentiles may glorify God for his mercy, as it is written, "Therefore I will praise you among the Gentiles; I will sing hymns to your name."

So prominent in the passion, Psalm 22 also describes Jesus' ministry today, worshiping the Father by his Spirit in the midst of the church:

Both the one who makes men holy and those who are made holy are of the same family. So Jesus is not ashamed to call them brothers. He says, "I will declare your name to my brothers; in the presence of the congregation I will sing your praises."[11]

Following Jesus' own example, the apostles were continually putting David's words into Jesus' mouth. Bearing in mind that the Gospels are not exhaustive histories, and recalling that the psalms most frequently cited (22 and 69) represent a substantial body of similar "psalms of individual lament," we can infer that this pattern was fuller than our record indicates.

Why This Pattern?

What justification did the apostles have for "reading Christ into" the Psalms in this way? Actually, they had a strong one. David himself, followed by the prophets, en-

---

11 Hebrews 2:11–12 (quoting Psalm 22:22); see also Acts 2:22–36 (quoting Psalm 16:10); Romans 15:8–9 (quoting Psalm 18:49).

couraged it. He knew that his reign did not stand in a vacuum, but pointed beyond itself to the reign of a great descendant.[12] God revealed this on the day of David's inauguration, when he promised him a son whose throne would last forever.[13]

But David was more than a king. He was a "man after God's own heart," a righteous prophet anointed by God to sing songs of covenant life. He foreshadowed the great Messiah, not only by virtue of his role as king, but also by virtue of his experience as the joyful worshiper, the faithful sufferer, and the vindicated servant.

For these reasons, Jews in Jesus' day readily assumed the legitimacy of applying David's words to the Messiah. A first-century rabbi might have disagreed with Peter's contention that "this Jesus" was the Christ.[14] But he would never have disagreed with the New Testament writers' habit of ascribing David's words to the Messiah (whoever he might be). Peter explains the pattern strikingly in his first epistle:

> The prophets, who spoke of the grace that was to come to you, searched intently and with the greatest care, trying to find out the time and circumstances to which the Spirit of Christ in them was pointing when he predicted the sufferings of Christ and the glories that would follow.[15]

---

12 See Psalms 110; 2; Isaiah 9:6–7.
13 2 Samuel 7:12–13.
14 Acts 2:36.
15 1 Peter 1:10–11.

The Old Testament prophets, including David, were themselves anointed by the Spirit of the "Anointed One" (the meaning of the Greek word *Christos*). He spoke of his own suffering and glory in theirs.

Rich New Meanings for Us

As we learn to listen in the Psalms for the voice of the Messiah, new depths of understanding open to us. For one thing, we come to appreciate the true humanity of our Lord more fully. The New Testament teaches that Jesus Christ was "in every respect . . . tempted as we are," that he "offered up prayers and supplications, with loud cries and tears, to him who was able to save him from death," and that he "learned obedience through what he suffered."[16] How, we ask with wonder, does the spotless Lamb of God learn anything, let alone obedience? The mystery of it is so great that we tend not to believe it, focusing our attention instead on the defense of the Savior's divinity and looking elsewhere for compassion and sympathy. Scholars argue that many Christians have fallen to the worship of Mary for this very reason; the notion of Christ's divinity distances him from our experience.

When we turn to the words of the Psalter and read them as Christ's very words, his humanity suddenly comes to life for us. We understand more fully what it means that our Lord submitted himself to the yoke of our flesh in order to redeem us. Read the words of Psalm 84:1–2—"How lovely is your dwelling place, O LORD Almighty! My soul yearns, even

---

16   Hebrews 4:15; 5:7–8.

faints, for the courts of the Lord"—and then picture Jesus at age twelve sitting with the rabbis in his Father's house, so captivated by his first visit to the temple that three days pass like so many hours. Hear the boy's quiet words of rebuke to his frantic parents, "Why were you searching for me? Didn't you know I had to be in my Father's house?" And then wonder with fresh insight at the words of Psalm 27:4, "One thing I ask of the Lord, this is what I seek: that I may dwell in the house of the Lord all the days of my life, to gaze upon the beauty of the Lord and to seek him in his temple."

Jesus understands human suffering. He struggled throughout his life with the inequities of human experience, seeing them more vividly that we ever have. Although he never gave in to unbelief and bitterness, the thought and words of Psalm 73:12–13 would have been a vehicle for his own:

> This is what the wicked are like—always carefree, they increase in wealth. Surely in vain have I kept my heart pure; in vain have I washed my hands in innocence.

Jesus knew the wounds of betrayal and desertion:

> Even my close friend, whom I trusted, he who shared my bread, has lifted up his heel against me.

> You have taken from me my closest friends and have made me repulsive to them.

My friends and companions avoid me because of my wounds; my neighbors stay far away.[17]

Jesus knew well the fear and loneliness that drive us in desperation to God for help. We can hear him in the Garden of Gethsemane pouring forth the words of Psalm 25:

> See how my enemies have increased and how fiercely they hate me! Guard my life and rescue me; let me not be put to shame, for I take refuge in you.[18]

Jesus knew, in the face of great suffering, the temptation to doubt God's love:

> Why are you so far from saving me, so far from the words of my groaning? O my God, I cry out by day, but you do not answer, by night, and am not silent.[19]

Jesus knew physical suffering and death:

> I am poured out like water, and all my bones are out of joint. My heart has turned to wax; it has melted away within me. My strength is dried up like a potsherd, and my tongue sticks to the roof of my mouth. . . . They have pierced my hands and my feet. I can count all my bones.[20]

17 Psalms 38:11 (cf. Mark 15:40); 41:9 (cf. John 13:18); 88:8 (cf. Mark 14:50).
18 Psalm 25:19–20.
19 Psalm 22:1–2.
20 Psalm 22:14–16.

Because he was fully human, Jesus knew even the afflictions brought on by sin. His sinless behavior did not exempt him from feeling the crushing weight of God's wrath, for "God made him who had no sin to be sin for us."[21] Viewed from this perspective, even the sinner's cries in the Psalms become his own:

> When I kept silent, my bones wasted away through my groaning all day long. For day and night your hand was heavy upon me; my strength was sapped as in the heat of summer.[22]

We can derive immense comfort from reading the Psalms as the word of our Mediator. Read this way, they remind us that there exists a man who lived for us the life that we should live, but fail to do so. There lives a man who loved to be continually in the courts of the Lord—unlike me. There lives a man who knows the full range of human suffering—better than I do. There lives a man whose sufferings were entirely undeserved—unlike mine. There lives a man who could say, "I wash my hands in innocence, and go about thy altar, O LORD, singing aloud a song of thanksgiving," a man with "clean hands and a pure heart,"[23] a man who could truly protest his full righteousness and innocence. That man was *not* David (Psalms 32 and 51 make this plain), and it certainly is not I. It is my great Redeemer, the

---

21   2 Corinthians 5:21.
22   Psalm 32:3–4.
23   Psalms 24:4; 26:6–7 RSV.

man Jesus, who not only died in my place, but also lived in my place.

The next time you read, "I was glad when they said to me, 'Let us go to the house of the LORD!' "[24] and are tempted to feel horribly guilty because you would rather be playing golf than worshiping God, remember that these are first and foremost the words of the one true Worshiper who fulfilled all righteousness on your behalf. More likely than not, when you perceive the matter this way, you will want to put your bags aside and go with thanks to praise the One who has so fully saved you.

Love Within the Godhead

There remains another benefit in reading the Psalms as the words of Christ. It lifts us out of ourselves and brings us to a high place from which we can view the entire drama of redemption from God's perspective. The most wondrous thing about the gospel is not what it does for us. Rather, it is what the gospel reveals about the love of the heavenly Father for his Son and the love of the Son for his Father.

The gospel reveals a divine Son who knows of his Father's holy love for a rebellious and perishing world and is zealous that all the cosmos should know and sing his Father's glory. And so he comes to us with the Father's blessing—indeed, according to the Father's plan—to restore in the example and mission of his own life the image of God's righteousness that we have so horribly marred. Driven by love for his Father, he lives every moment of his brief and

24   Psalm 122:1.

painful life to the honor of his Father's name. He submits to absolutely everything that the Father's righteousness requires, from the baptism of John to the baptism of death. And he does this knowing that by his death, offered in righteousness, he will reveal to the cosmos both his Father's absolute goodness in the punishment of sin and his Father's astonishing love in the redemption, at staggering personal cost, of sinners. The "joy set before him"[25] is not simply that of seeing us rescued. It is the joy of seeing all the lies about his Father's character and purposes, our lies and Satan's, overturned.

The love revealed in the drama of redemption flows with equal fervor in the other direction. The Father proclaims his zeal for his Son repeatedly by words from heaven ("This is my beloved Son. Hear him!") and by signs of great power. The Father comforts his Son by his word and ministers to him in prayer. But most vividly and cosmically, the Father exalts his Son in his passion and resurrection. The Cross reveals the wonder of Christ's infinite love for sinners and the Resurrection trumpets to principalities and powers, seen and unseen, that this Jesus is the deepest delight of his Father's heart. The resurrection of Jesus is the cosmic embrace of his Father, the declaration of his love and approval, like the explosive hug I gave my seven-year-old son when he scored his first goal in soccer, only infinitely more profound.

We can read many of the psalms, especially the psalms of individual lament, so as to see this cosmic drama. Some of these psalms, by virtue of their imagery, seem to demand

25   Hebrews 12:2.

that we read them this way. Take Psalm 18, for example. Written, according to its title, on the occasion of David's delivery from the hand of Saul, it lovingly praises God for delivering the psalmist from "the cords of death" and "the torrents of destruction." David remembers calling upon the Lord in his distress, and then he describes his deliverance in terms that clearly transcend his individual experience:

> The earth trembled and quaked, and the foundations of the mountains shook; they trembled because he was angry. Smoke arose from his nostrils; consuming fire came from his mouth. . . . He parted the heavens and came down; dark clouds were under his feet. . . . He shot his arrows and scattered the enemies, great bolts of lightning and routed them. The valleys of the sea were exposed and the foundations of the earth laid bare at your rebuke, O LORD, at the blast of breath from your nostrils. He reached down from on high and took hold of me; he drew me out of deep waters.[26]

When he wrote these words, David was certainly seeing something much grander than his own deliverance, something for which his experience was but a shadow. As we read these words, we think of the darkness that filled the sky and the earthquake that shook the environs of Jerusalem on Good Friday. And we anticipate the darkness and the shaking that are yet to be, when the Father's vindication of his Son is complete

26   Psalm 18:7–16.

and "every knee [shall] bow . . . and every tongue confess that Jesus Christ is Lord, to the glory of God the Father."[27]

David goes on to explain the reason for his rescue in terms that make us uncomfortable:

> He rescued me because he delighted in me. The LORD has dealt with me according to my righteousness; according to the cleanness of my hands he has rewarded me. For I have kept the ways of the LORD; I have not done evil by turning from my God. . . . I have been blameless before him and have kept myself from sin. The LORD has rewarded me according to my righteousness, according to the cleanness of my hands in his sight. To the faithful you show yourself faithful, to the blameless you show yourself blameless, to the pure you show yourself pure.[28]

Passages like this are embarrassing to read, particularly in the light of what we know of our Lord's teaching about the pervasiveness of sin. We may argue in our embarrassment that David had a sub-Christian grasp of the meaning of righteousness, or that he must have written this in the naïveté of youth, long before the Bathsheba episode. C. S. Lewis has gone so far as to say that such claims of self-righteousness led directly to the Pharisaism that Jesus so vehemently denounced.[29]

---

27 Philippians 2:10–11; Hebrews 12:26–29.

28 Psalm 18:19–26.

29 C. S. Lewis, *Reflections on the Psalms* (New York: Harcourt, Brace, and World, 1958), 17.

But when we set these words on Jesus' own lips, imagining him to be speaking them to his Father in the joy of Easter Sunday, they become precisely true and a source of great hope. The Father, furious over the suffering of his innocent Son, and delighted at his Son's flawless devotion through that suffering, lays the cosmos bare, overthrowing death itself in the zeal of his loving approval. The absolute righteousness of the Son calls forth an earthshaking deliverance from the Father.

As we read on in Psalm 18, we see even more of the love between Father and Son. The Son exults in the annihilation of the Evil One and joyfully acknowledges his Father's hand in the victory:

> I pursued my enemies and overtook them; I did not turn back till they were destroyed. . . . You armed me with strength for battle; you made my adversaries bow at my feet.

The Son receives from the Father's hand universal dominion:

> You have delivered me from the attacks of the people; you have made me the head of nations.

The Father delights to make his Son's triumph eternal:

> He gives his king great victories; he shows unfailing kindness to his anointed, to David and his descendants forever.

And the Son delights to sing his Father's praises before his people and before the world:

For who is God besides the LORD? And who is the Rock
except our God? . . . Therefore I will praise you among
the nations, O LORD; I will sing praises to your name.[30]

At the most profound theological level, worship is a
spectator sport. We gather to watch the Father vindicate his
Son in the preaching of the gospel and to watch the Son
give praise to his Father in the praises of our lips. For the
Spirit of Christ indwells us, and that Spirit lives to extol the
Father and the Son. This is perhaps the deepest meaning of
Zephaniah's ancient words:

Sing, O Daughter of Zion; shout aloud, O Israel! . . .
The LORD your God is with you. . . . He will take great
delight in you, he will quiet you with his love, he will
rejoice over you with singing.[31]

When next you gather for public worship, why not ask the
Lord to catch you up into the praises of the Godhead? Ask
him to give you in abundance the Spirit of Christ so that
your songs might be the songs of the One who loved his Father to the end, and your joy might be the joy of the Son
who was lifted from the tomb by the Father's embrace.

Questions for Discussion and Reflection

1. The image of the shepherd, which Jesus uses to describe himself (cf. John 10:2–5, 11–18; 21:15–17),
   frequently appears in the Psalms, sometimes as a de-

---

30 Psalm 18:37–39, 43, 50, 31, 49.
31 Zephaniah 3:14–17.

scription of the Lord (23; 80; 95:7) and sometimes as a description of David (78:70–72).

- What insights do these psalms give us into the character, person, and work of the Messiah?

2. Psalm 118 is the final psalm of the "Egyptian Hallel," sung to celebrate the Passover. Dramatic in form (various voices speak), it depicts a king returning victorious from the field of battle and demanding access to the city and the temple (v. 19) so that he may offer sacrifices to the Lord. This same psalm also figures prominently in the events surrounding Palm Sunday (vv. 25–26, cf. Matthew 21:9; vv. 22–23, cf. Matthew 21:42–43).

- What light does the drama of the psalm, given how it is used in the New Testament, shed on the meaning of the last week of Jesus' life?

3. Another image in the Psalms which Jesus takes to himself is that of the vine (80:8–18, cf. John 15:1–11).

- Compare the identity of the vine in Psalm 80 with the identity of the vine in John 15.

- What does this shift in identity teach us about Christ's role in our lives (cf. 1 Corinthians 15:22)?

- Why is this shift in identity important (cf. Isaiah 5:1–7)?

4. Look at Psalm 139:19–22. This section of an otherwise soothing psalm breathes the fire of zealous hatred against all who defy the Lord, and seems utterly inconsistent with the speech of Jesus, who prayed, "Father, forgive them, for they do not know what they are doing."

- What clue does Revelation 6:16–17 give us for understanding even such "imprecatory psalms" as his own words?

5. Psalm 96 and others like it foresee a day when the Lord himself will come, to the delight of the entire creation (cf. vv. 11–13).

- What great truth about the Messiah is hidden in this hope?
- When will this great advent be (read Romans 8:18–23 alongside Psalm 96)?
- How does Hebrews 2:5–9 deepen our understanding of the meditation on man in Psalm 8?

6. Read aloud the following psalms, as if Jesus Christ himself were speaking them. Alongside each psalm, list the attitude(s) or perspective(s) of Christ that the psalm illustrates. In addition, list particular events in Christ's ministry (past, present, or future) to which the words, attitudes, or perspectives give expression:

Psalms	Attitude(s) or Perspective(s)	Event(s)
2		
4:2		
23		
27:1–4		
51:8–12		
(cf. 2 Cor. 5:21;		
Heb. 4:15)		
69:1–4		
84		
101		
116:12–19		
119:113		

Chapter 8

BREAKING THE SILENCE

We have some friends who tried camping once with their two young children. They planned the weekend carefully, reserving their campsite well in advance and making sure they had all the equipment they would need. It was going to be a great time, the beginning of a great family tradition. Unfortunately, there were a number of unexpected problems. First, torrential rains fell on the night they left home. Second, because of the rain, they were delayed in traffic and did not arrive at the campsite until after the gate was closed. Mike had to hike through the downpour to find the gatekeeper. When they finally got in (the gatekeeper claimed that they had no reservation, "and, besides, you got here late, so reservations don't mean nothin'"), they had to set up their tent in the dark. Third, their one-year-old became violently sick, with vomiting and diarrhea throughout the night.

Life is full of disappointments and failed expectations. So often, hopes begin to take shape in our minds, only to be altered, sometimes violently, by experience. The Old Testament is like that. It is full of disappointing clashes between hope and experience, between promise and reality.

These clashes are no accident. God decreed them to point us toward his Son ("For no matter how many promises God has made, they are 'Yes' in Christ"). The Old Testament longs by design for the New. God planted the seeds of longing in the form of promises, allowing them to take root as the promises began to clash with the harsh realities of history. Finally, "when the time had fully come, God sent forth his Son" to bring all the tensions to a head and resolve them wondrously. Understanding this grand design, Jesus said,

> You diligently study the Scriptures because you think that by them you possess eternal life. These are the Scriptures that testify about me.[1]

Promises for a Broken World

God did not speak his promises in a vacuum. They were given in response to the profound needs occasioned by the Fall. Every relationship in life suffered from Adam's disobedience. Our relationship with God, initially open and intimate, became guilt-ridden and distant.[2] Our relationships

---

1 John 5:39; see 2 Corinthians 1:20; Galatians 4:4 RSV.
2 See Genesis 3:8–10. Adam and Eve hide from God, and, when confronted, Adam blames God for what has happened.

with each other, initially harmonious, became plagued by shame, blame shifting, jealousy, hatred, and division.[3] Nature, meant to submit happily and fruitfully to our labors, now yields only grudgingly and, in the end, kills us: "You are dust, and to dust you shall return."[4]

The deep and widespread upheaval of the Fall left us in great need of many things. First, we need to hear God's voice. Evicted from the garden, we wander aimlessly through a fallen world, cut off from the communion with God that we once knew. Second, we need pardon. Like Adam searching desperately for fig leaves, we need somehow to cover our shame, so that with a clear conscience we can approach God and one another. Third, we need love. We long for our world to be just, honest, peaceful, compassionate, and unified. Finally, we need somehow to overcome death and futility.

In the remaining chapters, we will consider the Old Testament's response to these needs, one at a time. We will see how the promises of old, when confronted by the reality of history, forced Old Testament believers to look for a solution that only Jesus Christ could bring.

Words from God

Have you ever felt the silence of God? Have you ever poured your heart out to him earnestly and repeatedly with no apparent results? Most of us have experienced this sort of

---

3 Adam and Eve hide from each other (3:7); Adam blames Eve for the Fall (3:12); Cain murders Abel (4:8); the nations are divided (11:8–9).

4 Genesis 3:17–19 RSV.

thing. Our ancestors in the Bible did, too. In the days of Elijah, for example, a devastating drought came over the land of Israel. People cried out to God for relief, but the heavens were like brass.[5]

This problem began in the Garden of Eden. When Adam and Eve disobeyed God, he cast them out of that place, cutting them off from the communion that they once knew.[6] But God kindly chose not to leave us in silence. Even after the Fall, he spoke to people. Cain, Enoch, Noah, Abraham, Hagar, Isaac, and Jacob all enjoyed verbal communication with God.

At the time of the Exodus, the Lord did something new. He gave his people Moses, the first great prophet:

> Listen to my words: When a prophet of the LORD is among you, I reveal myself to him in visions, I speak to him in dreams. But this is not true of my servant Moses; he is faithful in all my house. With him I speak face to face, clearly and not in riddles; he sees the form of the LORD.[7]

Moses stands out among all the prophets of Old Testament history. God gave him foundational responsibility, establish-

---

5 Cf. Deuteronomy 28:23. God spoke this curse through Elijah: "As the LORD the God of Israel lives, . . . there shall be neither dew nor rain these years, except by my word" (1 Kings 17:1 RSV).

6 Genesis 2:16–17 and 3:8 indicate that Adam and Eve enjoyed regular conversation with God prior to the Fall. No such conversations are on record following their eviction from the Garden of Eden.

7 Numbers 12:6–8.

ing Israel as a nation under his leadership. Through him, God gave Israel her "constitution," the Law of Moses.[8] With this responsibility came great privileges. Moses enjoyed direct verbal interaction with God (reminiscent of what Adam knew before the Fall) and was even privileged to see God without perishing.[9]

Through Moses, God made a great promise to Israel:

> The LORD your God will raise up for you a prophet like me from among your own brothers. You must listen to him. For this is what you asked of the LORD your God at Horeb on the day of the assembly when you said, "Let us not hear the voice of the LORD our God nor see this great fire anymore, or we will die." The LORD said to me: "What they say is good. I will raise up for them a prophet like you from among their brothers; I will put my words in his mouth, and he will tell them everything I command him."[10]

With these words, the Lord reassured Israel that when Moses died, they would not be left in the dark. God would establish a line of Hebrew prophets ("from among your own

---

8 That is, Genesis through Deuteronomy, also called the Pentateuch. Every other Old Testament writer based his work on this foundation. The Old Testament prophets are well described as prosecuting attorneys, holding the Law of Moses before the people.

9 Deuteronomy 34:10: "And there has not arisen a prophet since in Israel like Moses, whom the LORD knew face to face." See Exodus 33:18–23.

10 Deuteronomy 18:15–18.

brothers"), who would continue to serve them and protect them from the many diviners and spiritualists who populated Canaan. As Moses had done at Mount Sinai, when God first gave the Law, these prophets would shield the people from direct exposure to God's holy words, while at the same time getting the message across.

God promised further that this line of prophets would issue in one final prophet, a fellow Jew, who, like Moses, would stand between the people and God. He would reveal God fully ("He will tell them everything I command them"), and the people would obey him ("You must listen to him"). Isaiah frequently wrote in anticipation of this figure, often calling him the Servant of the Lord:

> Here is my servant, whom I uphold, my chosen one in whom I delight; I will put my Spirit on him and he will bring justice to the nations. . . .
>
> The Spirit of the Sovereign LORD is on me, because the LORD has anointed me to preach good news to the poor. He has sent me to bind up the brokenhearted, to proclaim freedom for the captives and release from darkness for the prisoners, to proclaim the year of the LORD's favor and the day of vengeance of our God.[11]

Problems with the Prophets

Difficulties surfaced from the beginning. Not even Moses represented God perfectly. On one of the occasions when

---

11   Isaiah 42:1; 61:1–2.

thirsty Israel threatened the leader in the wilderness, the Lord commanded him to assemble the congregation and to "speak to that rock before their eyes and it will pour out its water." Instead, Moses angrily rebuked the people and struck the rock twice with his staff. To this God responded,

> Because you did not trust in me enough to honor me as holy in the sight of the Israelites, you will not bring this community into the land I give them.[12]

God's response may mystify us (in another setting, the Lord had commanded Moses to strike the rock).[13] What is plain is that Moses' behavior misrepresented God before the people and led the Lord to bar him from the Promised Land. Not even his intimacy with the Lord kept Moses from failure in his calling.

Godly prophets served ancient Israel, especially at the early and final stages of her national history.[14] They faithfully prosecuted their call, speaking the word without compromise, even when it was painful to do so. Samuel exemplified this spirit. He loved King Saul, having found,

---

12 Numbers 20:2–13.

13 Exodus 17:1–7. Many see this story as a picture of the crucifixion, in which the Lord (represented by the rock—see 1 Corinthians 10:4) is struck in our place so that we might have life. To strike God, even at his express command, is shocking. To do it without such a command (as in Numbers 20) is unthinkable. To do it more than once is to suggest that the crucifixion was insufficient.

14 Moses and Samuel stand out in the early years. Many of the later prophets (Amos, Obadiah, etc.) committed their prophecies to writing, which we find in the Old Testament.

anointed, and counseled him, but when Saul proved un-
faithful, Samuel brokenheartedly abandoned him: "Until
the day Samuel died, he did not go to see Saul again, though
Samuel mourned for him."[15]

Sadly, good prophets like Samuel arose only infre-
quently, and, since they were only human, the benefits of
their work did not endure.

Many false prophets fill the pages of Israel's history, continually undermining the faithful ones. Two vivid stories tell
us much. When Jehoshaphat and Ahab, the kings of Judah
and Israel, contemplate riding together in battle against a foreign enemy, they seek counsel. Ahab's four hundred prophets
promise victory. When asked by Jehoshaphat if there are any
prophets of the Lord present, Ahab responds testily,

> There is still one man through whom we can inquire
> of the LORD, but I hate him because he never prophe-
> sies anything good about me, but always bad. He is
> Micaiah son of Imlah.

As expected, Micaiah opposes the four hundred in the name
of the Lord, and goes to prison for his stand. In the disaster
that follows, Ahab loses not only the battle, but his life.[16]

Elijah shares Micaiah's experience. Arrayed on Mount
Carmel against 450 prophets of Baal, all of whom enjoy the
king's favor, Elijah cries out in desperate solitude, "I am the
only one left."[17]

---

15   1 Samuel 15:35.
16   2 Chronicles 18.
17   1 Kings 19:10.

False prophecy abounded so much in Israel and Judah that God's true heralds constantly cried out against it. Here is a sampling:

> The prophets are prophesying lies in my name. I have not sent them or appointed them or spoken to them. They are prophesying to you false visions, divinations, idolatries and the delusions of their own minds. . . . Those same prophets will perish by sword and famine.

> The visions of your prophets were false and worthless; they did not expose your sin to ward off your captivity. The oracles they gave you were false and misleading.

> Woe to the foolish prophets who follow their own spirit and have seen nothing! Your prophets, O Israel, are like jackals among ruins. You have not gone up to the breaks in the wall to repair it for the house of Israel so that it will stand firm in the battle on the day of the LORD. . . . They lead my people astray, saying, "Peace," when there is no peace, and because, when a flimsy wall is built, they cover it with whitewash. . . . So I will spend my wrath against the wall and against those who covered it with whitewash. I will say to you, "The wall is gone and so are those who whitewashed it, those prophets of Israel who prophesied to Jerusalem and saw visions of peace for her when there was no peace," declares the Sovereign LORD.[18]

18 Jeremiah 14:14–15; Lamentations 2:14; Ezekiel 13:3–5, 10–11, 15–16.

God had established the office of prophet so that his people could escape the confusion of diviners and spiritualists in Canaan. But many Hebrew "seers" turned out to be as bad as their pagan counterparts. Called to speak God's mind, they proclaimed only the confusion of their own. Called as prosecuting attorneys to remind the people of God's holy law and the consequences of breaking it, they spoke of peace when there was no peace. Called to protect God's people with the truth, they allowed deception to penetrate the kingdom and became little more than scavengers ("jackals") in the ruins left behind.

Problems with the People

False prophets were only half the problem. The people of Israel, who hard-heartedly and routinely refused to listen to the many good prophets God sent, contributed fully to the tragedy. And they did so from the start. Israel was still at Sinai, having just received the Ten Commandments (Moses was still conferring with the Lord on the mountain), when Aaron melted their golden earrings and molded them into a golden calf, declaring:

> These are your gods, O Israel, who brought you up out of Egypt. . . . Tomorrow there will be a festival to the LORD.

The people repeatedly despised and threatened Moses in the wilderness. Aaron's complaint was typical: "Has the LORD spoken only through Moses?"[19]

---

19 Numbers 12:2. Exodus 32 describes the golden calf incident. See Numbers 14:1–10, 39–45; 16:1–35, 41–50; 20:1–13; 21:4–9.

From first to last, the kings were hardly better than the people. Saul disobeyed Samuel's explicit command to destroy the Amalekites and "repented" only when he saw that his action cost him the throne. Zedekiah, the last king of Judah, saw Jerusalem destroyed and went into exile because

> he did evil in the eyes of the LORD, just as Jehoiakim had done. It was because of the LORD's anger that all this happened to Jerusalem and Judah, and in the end he thrust them from his presence.[20]

Ignoring God's word is bad enough. The people often went much further, attacking the message and the messengers. They often condemned true prophets as liars, a vivid example of which occurred toward the end of Jeremiah's life. A small group of rebels murdered Gedaliah, the puppet king set up by Nebuchadnezzar after the destruction of Judah. Knowing that the king of Babylon would soon descend in fury upon them, they asked Jeremiah for God's wisdom on whether they should flee to Egypt or stay put:

> May the LORD be a true and faithful witness against us if we do not act in accordance with everything the LORD your God sends you to tell us. Whether it is favorable or unfavorable, we will obey the LORD our God, to whom we are sending you, so that it will go well with us, for we will obey the LORD our God.

20 2 Kings 24:18–20. First Samuel 15 describes the fall of King Saul.

Jeremiah told them to stay and submit to God's discipline through Nebuchadnezzar. But what was their response?

> You are lying! The LORD our God has not sent you to say, "You must not go to Egypt to settle there."[21]

Another favorite assault was Scripture twisting—bending and editing the prophets' words so as to avoid their central intent:

> For day after day they seek me out; they seem eager to know my ways, as if they were a nation that does what is right. . . . Your fasting ends in quarreling and strife, and in striking each other with wicked fists.[22]

But not even twisting was enough at times. Like so many in our day, the people in ancient Israel cried out for lies:

> They say to the seers, "See no more visions!" and to the prophets, "Give us no more visions of what is right! Tell us pleasant things, prophesy illusions. Leave this way, get off this path, and stop confronting us with the Holy One of Israel!"[23]

If the prophet would not oblige, there were of course the options of imprisonment and murder. When Herod

---

21   Jeremiah 42:5–6; 43:2.
22   Isaiah 58:2, 4; see also Isaiah 1:1–17; Malachi 1; 3. Jesus brings the same charge in Matthew 23:23–24.
23   Isaiah 30:10–11. The problem is still with us (see 2 Timothy 4:3–4).

threw John the Baptist into jail, he was following in the dubious tradition of men like Ahab, who did the same to Micaiah. Jezebel, Ahab's wife, had a better idea. On the occasion of Elijah's great victory over the prophets of Baal, she vowed that within twenty-four hours she would kill him.[24]

Think about Jeremiah's situation. He had before him the great promise of Deuteronomy 18. He also knew the eight hundred years of history that had unfolded after that promise was made. Most prophets had lied, and the people had despised those who were faithful. Is it any wonder that Jeremiah has been called "the weeping prophet"?

The Word Made Flesh

Jeremiah's tears were not in vain. They fell as the Spirit of Christ yearned within him for the day when the eternal Word would take on human flesh, the day we celebrate every year at Christmas:

> And the Word became flesh and dwelt among us, full of grace and truth; we have beheld his glory, glory as of the only Son from the Father.

Jesus saw himself as the perfect and final fulfillment of the promise of a prophet made in Deuteronomy 18, and his disciples concurred in that judgment.[25] And well they might,

---

24 1 Kings 19:1–2.

25 John 1:14 RSV. First Peter 1:11 tells us that "the Spirit of Christ" was speaking in the prophets. Philip (John 1:45), Stephen (Acts 7:37), Peter (Acts 3:22–23), and Jesus (John 5:45–47; 12:48–50) all applied Deuteronomy 18 to Jesus.

since Jesus was a prophet who was more than a prophet. He was (and is) divine, speaking the truth because he was (and is) the truth. In one way or another, he repeatedly made this claim:

> I am the light of the world. Whoever follows me will never walk in darkness, but will have the light of life.

> I am the way and the truth and the life. No one comes to the Father except through me.[26]

How startlingly Jesus fulfilled God's promise to put his words into the mouth of his prophet! In the case of Moses, Elijah, Jonah, and all the other great prophets, their messages were "from outside"—alien. But Jesus' words were "from inside" because of who he was.

And what gracious words they were! When God first spoke at Mount Sinai, Israel cringed in terror. The Israelites begged Moses to be their go-between, so they would not have to face God directly. Jesus Christ removes this "buffer," bringing God directly to us in his every word and gesture, and yet for some reason (see the next chapter) the experience does not undo us:

> You are the most excellent of men and your lips have been anointed with grace, since God has blessed you forever.

26 John 8:12; 14:6.

For the law was given through Moses; grace and truth came through Jesus Christ.[27]

Jesus' words are more than kind and true. They are complete, all we need to know (and more) to be restored to living fellowship with God:

> In the past God spoke to our forefathers through the prophets at many times and in various ways, but in these last days he has spoken to us by his Son. . . . The Son is the radiance of God's glory and the exact representation of his being.

Do you really want to know God? Look at the Jesus revealed in the Bible. He has the Father's likeness, because he is the Father's Son. In Jesus Christ, we get more than bits and snatches. We get the whole wonderful reality (certainly all we need now): "He who has seen me has seen the Father."[28]

Ears to Hear

Jesus solves the other problem with prophesy. Remember, Jeremiah wept not only because the prophets were corrupt. He did so also because the people would not listen. Our great Prophet enters and changes us inwardly, just as Ezekiel had predicted:

---

27 Psalm 45:2; John 1:17. The psalm prophesies the gracious character of the Messiah's speech. See also Hebrews 12:18–24, especially v. 24.

28 John 14:9 RSV; Hebrews 1:1–3 describes Christ's superiority over the prophets.

117

I will give you a new heart and put a new spirit in you; I will remove from you your heart of stone and give you a heart of flesh. And I will put my Spirit in you and move you to follow my decrees and be careful to keep my laws.

Is this not what happens when a person is born again? She does not suddenly stop sinning, of course, but a profound inward change occurs, so that she can say, like the apostle Paul, "I delight in the law of God, in my inmost self." She no longer wants to live as she once did. This is the point of so many of Jesus' healing miracles. When he restores sight to the blind and hearing to the deaf, he proclaims in effect, "I have come to change the heart, so that you can finally understand and receive my ways."[29]

What God starts, he finishes: "He who began a good work in you will bring it to completion at the day of Jesus Christ."[30] Ancient Israel was on occasion open to the Lord, but seemed inevitably to fall away. Not even Israel's finest kings escaped. The wonderful news brought to us by our Prophet is that we will in the end make it. We are his workmanship, and God never leaves anything half done.

Prophets One and All

But the Spirit of Christ does even more than make his people receptive to the final revelation that Jesus brings. He

---

29 Ezekiel 36:26–27; Romans 7:22 RSV. John 8:12–9:41 treats Jesus' healing of a blind man as proof that he is "the light of the world."

30 Philippians 1:6 RSV.

makes us all prophets of God, bearers of the message that transforms the world. This is the point of Peter's use of Joel's prophecy on the Day of Pentecost:

> In the last days, God says, I will pour out my Spirit on all people. Your sons and daughters will prophesy, your young men will see visions, your old men will dream dreams. Even on my servants, both men and women, I will pour out my Spirit in those days, and they will prophesy.

From the moment Adam blamed Eve for his failure, our race has filled history with lies. Beginning with God's promise to raise up prophets "from among you," the Old Testament longed for a time of universal truth-telling. Moses cried in exasperation, "I wish that all the LORD's people were prophets and that the LORD would put his Spirit on them!" Solomon declared, "The mouth of the righteous is a fountain of life." Isaiah and Habakkuk saw a day when "the earth will be full of the knowledge of the LORD as the waters cover the sea." Joel saw a time when young and old, male and female—"all people"—would tell forth God's truth abundantly and exuberantly.[31]

While we still await the final expression of this vision, its fulfillment has already begun. If you are a Christian, regardless of your age, gender, social status, race, or training, your words can be "a fountain of life." For the Spirit who

---

31 Peter quotes Joel 2:28–32 in Acts 2:17–18. See Numbers 11:29; Proverbs 10:11 (also 13:14; 18:4–5); Isaiah 11:9; Habakkuk 2:14.

filled Jesus and the prophets before him lives in you. This perhaps helps us to understand something of what Jesus meant when he promised that we would do "greater things" than he did during his earthly ministry.

Running from the Light

Our world is full of people searching for the truth. And yet that search is full of paradoxes and contradictions. Many (like the ancient Israelites) are willing to try almost anything except the God of the Bible—crystals, gurus of every sort, naturalistic science. Those who are not deeply committed to some "truth fad" tend to be convinced that, if there is any absolute truth, it is not knowable. Modern physics and the sheer volume of things as yet unexplored in the cosmos feed this sense of skepticism. Still others in our day, keenly aware of religious pluralism, hold passionately to the notion that absolute, knowable religious truth does not exist. It is somehow unfair, undemocratic, even immoral, to be exclusive about religion.

Into this cultural scene comes the Bible—more to the point, the God of the Bible and his Son. He loves this lost world and desires to enter into fellowship with its people. For this reason, as we might reasonably expect, he has spoken to us in human language and finally in human form. It is a wonderful thing. But the fact that so many resist him, the fact that so many dismiss on principle the notion of accessible revelation, the fact that so few take the time to read the prophets and to meet the great Prophet, is an unspeakable tragedy.

It is also a great opportunity. By what we say and how we

live, we can demonstrate that there is in fact Truth and that he can be known. We have a message—Paul calls it "the power of God unto salvation"—which has transformed people and cultures, and can do so again, if only we will speak it:

> But you are a chosen people, a royal priesthood, a holy nation, a people belonging to God, *that you may declare* the praises of him who called you out of darkness into his wonderful light.[32]

Questions for Discussion and Reflection

1. Read Deuteronomy 18:9–22.
   a. According to this passage, what problem in Canaan did God send the prophets to clear up?
   b. Can you think of any modern "soothsayers"?
   c. According to the passage, how can we identify a true prophet of God? Where are they to be found today?
   d. What should characterize our response to a true prophet?
   e. How did (or does) Jesus fulfill the description of a prophet given here?
2. Read Numbers 20:2–13.
   a. What did God ask Moses to do?
   b. How did Moses misrepresent God?
   c. Why was the punishment so harsh (see footnote 13)?
3. Read Jeremiah 14:14–15, Lamentations 2:14, and Ezekiel 13:3–7; 16:16.

32 1 Peter 2:9.

   a. What sorts of crimes, specifically, were the prophets guilty of, according to these passages?

   b. Where do we see the same problems today, both in the church and in the world?

4. The response of Israel to God's prophets was amply illustrated in the wilderness. Look over Numbers 12; 14:1–10, 39–45; 16:1–35, 41–50; 20:1–13; 21:4–9. Zero in on Korah's rebellion (16:1–35).

   a. How is Korah's attitude in 16:3 typical of the attitude many people have toward the Bible today?

   b. What happened to Korah and his followers?

   c. Does this seem unnecessarily violent to you? Why or why not?

5. Consider 1 Samuel 15.

   a. What terms does Samuel use to describe the instructions given to Saul?

   b. What does this teach about Samuel's understanding of his authority?

   c. Notice how Saul seeks to get out from under the commandment (vv. 14–15, 20–21). How might we do the same?

6. Read John 14:15–18, 25–26; 15:26; 16:5–15.

   a. What prophetic ministries did Jesus promise that the Holy Spirit would have in the lives of his disciples?

   b. In what ways are these promises the same for us, and in what ways were they unique to the apostles? (Hint: Is the New Testament a loose-leaf notebook? Also see Ephesians 2:20.)

   c. Where do we see the fulfillment of these promises?

7. Jesus Christ fulfills the longing of the Old Testament for clear communication from God. Each of the following sets of passages describes a different aspect of that fulfillment. Look up at least one passage from each set:

   - Ezekiel 36:26–27; Romans 7:22; Philippians 1:6
   - John 1:14; John 14:9; Hebrews 1:1–4
   - Proverbs 10:11; Isaiah 11:9; Acts 2:17–18

   a. How, according to each passage, have things improved for you, for the church, and (potentially at least) for the world, now that Christ has come?

   b. Spend some time thanking Christ for his prophetic ministry.

Chapter 9

DARING TO DRAW NEAR

I remember speaking once with a young teenager in my church who had been caught shoplifting. An electronic surveillance device had detected the stolen goods as he attempted to leave the store, automatically locking the door and issuing the polite but ominous command: "Please report to a store clerk immediately!" The store owner eventually let the young man off, but not until he had publicly humiliated and terrified him, demanding that he never set foot in the shop again. As the teen left, shoppers jeered at him.

Getting caught had clearly unnerved my young friend, so much so that by the time he saw me three months later, he still did not have the courage to tell his parents about it. Humiliation, guilt, and fear hung heavily upon him.

Ever since the catastrophe in the Garden of Eden, we have lived in fear of getting caught. Adam's behavior typifies our own. A creature who had only recently enjoyed God's company was suddenly afraid of him, hiding at the sound of his approach. Attempting in vain to cover his guilt, he responded to God's probing questions by blaming both God and his wife: "The woman you put here with me—she gave me some fruit from the tree, and I ate it." Eve followed suit, shifting blame to the serpent.[1]

People deal with their bad consciences in many ingenious ways. Some practice denial by keeping themselves busy working or entertaining themselves (cable TV and video movies can easily fill every leisure hour with nonreflective stimulation). Others try to balance off the bad stuff with religious or philanthropic activity. Still others attempt (subconsciously) to purge their guilt by vigorously condemning similar failures in other people (I can often identify my own problems by asking what makes me most angry in other people's behavior). Another common approach to the problem is to develop a philosophy or a psychology that denies the existence of true guilt. Guilt is a feeling, many say, conceived by religious myth or imposed arbitrarily during childhood.

We are adept at blaming anything and anyone other than ourselves—the school board, the government, our parents, our children, the environment. When my sister confronted her son for biting his little brother, he said, "But mama, his hand was in my mouth when my teeth were closing." Caught in an outright lie during the Watergate scandal, one of the White House functionaries said, "That former statement is inoperable."

Such ingenuity often makes us laugh. But what it reveals of the profound difficulty we have coming clean alarms us.

1   Genesis 3:8–13.

We lie about ourselves because we are afraid. We cannot survive a careful scrutiny.

Our guilt and fear, though sometimes misdirected, are not just "in our heads." God cast Adam and Eve out of the Garden and set the cherubim to guard its gates because their problem was real, not just a matter of feelings in need of a change. Isaiah says, "Your iniquities have separated you from your God; your sins have hidden his face from you, so that he will not hear."[2] Not only are we driven from God by our rebellion, but he is also driven from us; his holy character cannot bear anything that is unholy.

God's goodness is like the sun's heat. We cannot approach either one without perishing. We see this at Mount Sinai, when God gave the Law to his newly delivered people:

> On the morning of the third day there was thunder and lightning, with a thick cloud over the mountain, and a very loud trumpet blast. Everyone in the camp trembled. . . . Mount Sinai was covered with smoke, because the LORD descended on it in fire. . . . The whole mountain trembled violently, and the sound of the trumpet grew louder and louder. Then Moses spoke and the voice of God answered him. . . . And the LORD said to him, "Go down and warn the people so that they do not force their way through to see the LORD and many of them perish."[3]

2   Isaiah 59:2.
3   Exodus 19:16, 18–19, 21.

God is "a consuming fire," whose goodness must and will burn off all that is impure, including us. Not even the great Bible heroes escaped this. Meeting God in a vision, Isaiah cried out in horror, "Woe to me! I am ruined!" He psychologically came apart at the seams in the presence of God's majesty. Ezekiel, Daniel, and even the beloved disciple John fell to the ground as dead men when they saw God's glory.[4]

The Old Testament "Solution"

God intervened from the beginning to give us hope. Within moments of the Fall, he covered Adam's and Eve's shame, providing animal skins for their naked bodies.[5] Many years later he "covered" his chosen people's shame in a similar way, through an elaborate priestly system, at the heart of which was substitutionary animal sacrifice. Through this system, God aimed to bring his people close.

God's priests served as go-betweens, bringing the people to God. They made people and things holy for God's service—anointing kings, cleansing lepers and new mothers, and cleansing instruments of worship.[6] Most importantly, they presided over a sacrificial system aimed at enhancing fellowship with God and devotion to him.

The Old Testament describes at least six different types of offerings (burnt, grain, sin, guilt, fellowship, and drink).[7] Some (like the sin and guilt offerings) were prescribed un-

---

4 Isaiah 6:5; Ezekiel 1:29; Daniel 7:28; 8:27; Revelation 1:17.
5 Genesis 3:21.
6 Exodus 29:37; Leviticus 12:6–8; 14; 16:15–16, 18–19; 1 Kings 1:39.
7 Leviticus 1–7 details most of these.

der certain circumstances. God required these to pay for sin and turn away his wrath.[8] Others—the burnt, grain, fellowship, and drink offerings—seem to have been spontaneous, offered freely in response to God's faithfulness. Some, notably the burnt offerings (called "holocausts" by some), were consumed in their entirety "to signify that the gift was total and irrevocable."[9] Still others (like the grain offerings) were communal meals, with parts of the offering going to God, the priests, and the offerers. God invited families to eat their own tithes joyfully in his presence and to share them with the Levites.[10] Whatever the particulars, the need for open and happy fellowship with God drove the sacrificial system.

The tabernacle most vividly portrayed God's plan. Desiring to live with and bless his people, God had them build him a movable house, designed to go with them wherever they went.[11] When Israel settled later in the Promised Land, God abandoned his tent for a more permanent house (the temple), but the purpose was the same. He made his presence obvious by filling both structures with his glory cloud at the moment of their dedications. The Israelites understandably prayed toward these "houses" (the tabernacle was called "the Tent of Meeting"), and, once settled in Canaan,

8   Leviticus 16 orders a variety of sin and guilt offerings on the annual Day of Atonement. See also Leviticus 4; 5:14–6:7.

9   Xavier Leon-Dufour, *Dictionary of Biblical Theology* (New York: Seabury Press, 1967), 513. See Leviticus 1:13.

10   Leviticus 2:9–10 details the grain offerings and Deuteronomy 12:17–19; 14:22–27 the sharing and enjoyment of the tithes.

11   "Have them make a sanctuary for me, and I will dwell among them" (Exodus 25:8).

went on yearly pilgrimages to the temple. In exile, they longed for the temple because they longed for God.[12]

The Historical Reality

The priestly system proved disappointing. For one thing, the priests failed in their appointed task. Even as Moses was receiving the Law at Mount Sinai, Aaron—the first high priest—was leading the people in the worship of a golden calf. Aaron's sons were no better, offering "unholy fire" and perishing in the attempt. Ezekiel accused the priests of his time of "doing violence to [God's] law and profaning [his] holy things . . . making no distinction between the holy and the common."

Micah railed against their greed and personal interest. On at least one occasion, a priest beat Jeremiah in order to silence his preaching. Not even the experience of exile seemed to do much good: the priests of Malachi's day avoided God, taught falsehood, and encouraged spiritual sloth by their own attitude.[13]

On rare occasions, faithful priests emerged. Samuel served in a number of roles, including a priestly one, and did so with a heart set on God's honor. Despite his failure with the golden calf, Aaron proved generally faithful. One brave priest gave refuge to David during his wilderness wan-

---

12 Exodus 25–27 describes the tabernacle. Exodus 40:34 and 1 Kings 8:10–11 depict the awesome filling of the tabernacle and the temple by the glory cloud. First Kings 8:31–32 and Psalm 84:1–4 evidence Israel's conviction that the temple was God's abode.

13 Leviticus 10:1–2; Jeremiah 20:1–6; Ezekiel 23:26; Micah 3:11; Malachi 2:1–9.

derings, despite great personal danger. Sadly, some of these men, like David's protector, died violently because of their faithfulness.[14]

The people abused the system as fully as the priests did. They profaned the sanctuary, bringing lame and blind animals for worship and withholding the tithe.[15] They continually made a pretence of worship, going through the motions while their hearts and lives were distant and disobedient. Isaiah declared God's displeasure:

> "The multitude of your sacrifices—what are they to me?" says the LORD. "I have more than enough of burnt offerings, of rams and the fat of fattened animals; I have no pleasure in the blood of bulls and lambs and goats. . . . Your New Moon festivals and your appointed feasts my soul hates. . . . Your hands are full of blood; wash and make yourselves clean. Take your evil deeds out of my sight! Stop doing wrong, learn to do right! Seek justice, encourage the oppressed. Defend the cause of the fatherless, plead the case of the widow."[16]

Even before human hypocrisy wrecked the priestly system, its inadequacy showed. Although God lived with his people, he was still distant from them. Blood sacrifice dominated religious life, declaring with each new day the persis-

---

14   1 Samuel 21:1–6; 22:9–19.

15   Malachi 1:6–10; 2:11; 3:9–10.

16   Isaiah 1:11, 14, 15–17.

tence of sin. The design of the tabernacle had a similar effect. The Holy of Holies, where God dwelt, was sealed from the rest of the tabernacle by a thick curtain. No one could enter it, on pain of death, except the high priest. And the high priest could do this only once a year, on the Day of Atonement, and then only after an elaborate ritual of cleansing. Uzzah's shocking death in David's time reinforced the obvious—God was too close for comfort.[17]

The final blow to Israel's hopes came when Jerusalem fell to the Babylonians in 589 B.C.:

> [Nebuchadnezzar] carried to Babylon all the articles from the temple of God, both large and small, and the treasures of the LORD's temple. . . . [He] set fire to God's temple and broke down the wall of Jerusalem. . . . He carried into exile to Babylon the remnant, who escaped from the sword, and they became servants of him and his sons.[18]

Imagine living through this when it happened. Cruel and unbelieving strangers violate and then destroy God's house, carrying away all its treasures. They handle the ark as Uzzah did, but unlike him they are unharmed. They kill off most of your family, and then carry you away to a foreign place to be their slave for the rest of your life. Where is God? Has he

17 In an effort to keep the ark of the covenant from falling off a cart during its transportation to Jerusalem, Uzzah reached out and touched it. He died instantly. See 1 Chronicles 13.

18 2 Chronicles 36:18–20.

left his house and his people forever? If somehow he remains in the land, what good is it to you, since you have been carried off to a distant place? Doubt and despair haunt you as you contemplate what seems to be God's repudiation of his people and of his own system for bringing them close. It would appear that you are no better off than the pagans you have so often judged.

Jesus Christ: the One Who Brings Us Near

Reality seemed to belie the promises. God's nearness through the priestly system served ironically to accentuate his distance. Human failure transformed God's presence from a blessing to a curse. Alert to the depth of this problem, the prophets longed for a radical divine solution. Isaiah envisioned a human lamb, morally without blemish, commissioned by God as a guilt offering in our place:

> But he was pierced for our transgressions, he was crushed for our iniquities; the punishment that brought us peace was upon him, and by his wounds we are healed. We all, like sheep, have gone astray, each of us has turned to his own way; and the LORD has laid on him the iniquity of us all.[19]

Zechariah saw God stripping the high priest Joshua of his "filthy garments," despite Satan's furious accusations, and replacing them "with rich apparel." He foresaw a day when God's reality would so dominate Jewish life that horse bri-

---

19   Isaiah 53:4–6.

dles would be inscribed "Holy to the LORD" and common cookware throughout the nation would be as sacred as "the bowls before the altar."[20] Malachi soberly anticipated a bright future:

> "See, I will send my messenger, who will prepare the way before me. Then suddenly the Lord you are seeking will come to his temple; the messenger of the covenant, whom you desire, will come." . . . But who can endure the day of his coming? Who can stand when he appears? For he will be like a refiner's fire. . . . He will purify the Levites. . . . Then the LORD will have men who will bring offerings in righteousness, and the offerings of Judah and Jerusalem will be acceptable to the LORD.[21]

God himself would clean up the priestly system by cleaning up the priests themselves.

We see more clearly than Malachi how God did it. He came as the man Jesus to live with us and to purify our lives and worship:

> The Word became flesh and made his dwelling [or "tabernacled"] among us.

> Therefore, brothers, since we have confidence to enter the Most Holy Place by the blood of Jesus, by

20 Zechariah 3:1–4 RSV; 14:20–21 RSV.
21 Malachi 3:1–4.

a new and living way opened for us through the curtain, that is, his body, and since we have a great priest over the house of God, let us draw near to God with a sincere heart in full assurance of faith, having our hearts sprinkled to cleanse us from a guilty conscience and having our bodies washed with pure water.[22]

Jesus Christ closed the gap between God and people. He became one of us in order to offer himself in our place as a flawless sacrifice of praise and atonement. In the language of the book of Hebrews, he opened the way through the thick "curtain" that separated people from the Holy of Holies, enabling them to commune unafraid with God.

The Shadow and the Reality

God intended the entire priestly system—the temple, the tabernacle, the priestly rituals, and the sacrifices—to foreshadow (cf. Hebrews 10:1) his plan for removing human guilt and fear. The tabernacle depicted heaven—"the greater and more perfect tent (not made with hands, that is, not of this creation)." The Holy of Holies, with its carved cherubim over the ark (or mercy seat), portrayed the throne room of God at the center of heaven. The elaborate cleansings required of the priests and the articles of worship emphasized both the inaccessibility of God and the hope that he might somehow be approached. The grain of-

22 John 1:14; Hebrews 10:19–22.

ferings and the altar of incense spoke of the prayer- and praise-filled obedience that should flow continually from our hearts.[23]

The sacrificial offerings (the scapegoats, the countless bulls and rams, and the Passover lambs) spoke of a cleansing from the defilement of sin that they themselves could not accomplish. Our consciences forever whisper that "it is impossible for the blood of bulls and goats to take away sins."[24] Only man could pay for man's guilt, and so the real sacrifice had to be human.

But the sacrifices had to be without spot or blemish, pointing to a sacrifice that was more than human. Like no one before or since, Jesus lived his life for God. He grew up in the real world, where "he learned obedience through what he suffered." He faced every temptation we face, without giving in. On the eve of his death, he was a fully proven man, a flawless priest possessing in himself a flawless offering. He made that offering at the cross, presenting himself as both priest and victim for the purpose of reconciling us to God in one mighty and effectual act.[25]

Jesus' fulfillment of the old system takes our breath away. As we have seen, he satisfied in unprecedented depth the requirements of the sin offering. We often miss his fulfillment of the other offerings as well. He freely chose the Incarnation and the Cross in trusting devotion to his Father, just as Jews of old freely chose their grain and fellow-

---

23 Hebrews 8–10; see especially 8:5; 9:8, 11 RSV, 24; 10:1.

24 Hebrews 10:4; see Exodus 12; Leviticus 16.

25 Hebrews 4:15; 5:8–9 RSV; 9:11–14.

ship offerings. In other words, his entire life was a freewill offering, a "fragrant offering and sacrifice to God."[26] Further, he chose to be a burnt offering, withholding nothing of himself from the altar of God. Zeal for God's house drove him in life and in death, consuming him utterly.[27] No one can fathom the experience of spiritual annihilation behind Jesus' words, "My God, my God, why have you forsaken me?" for no one has ever known God as Jesus did, nor has any living man or woman ever experienced hell in its fullness.

Jesus' self-offering was above all a communal meal where he called his disciples (and us) to celebrate together joyfully in his provision. His very life, the bread of heaven, has replaced the firstfruits of the earth and welcomed us to a permanent communion that will continue beyond the grave:[28]

> And so, Jesus' offering, in its bloody reality and in its sacramental expression, sums up and fulfills the sacrificial economy of the OT: it is at once a holocaust, expiatory offering, and sacrifice of communion. . . . Old terminology, new content. The reality transcends the categories of thought which serve to express it.[29]

---

26 Ephesians 5:2, using Old Testament language. Leviticus especially describes God's response to freewill offerings in this way. See 1:9, 17, etc.

27 John 2:17, where Psalm 69:9 is cited as descriptive of Jesus' ministry.

28 See John 6:53–58; 1 Corinthians 10:16.

29 Leon-Dufour, *Dictionary of Biblical Theology*, 514.

Rich Benefits for Us

As Jesus died, the temple shook, and the veil separating God's "throne room" from the rest of the building tore from top to bottom. God could not have spoken more clearly: "We can be close now. You can be honest with me about sin, and we can begin to deal with it, because I have fully punished it." The letter to the Hebrews explains:

> The blood of goats and bulls and the ashes of a heifer sprinkled on those who are ceremonially unclean sanctify them so that they are outwardly clean. How much more, then, will the blood of Christ, who through the eternal Spirit offered himself unblemished to God, cleanse our consciences from acts that lead to death, so that we may serve the living God![30]

Notice that the Cross does not set us free for sin; it sets us free from sin. The work of Jesus liberates us from the fear of condemnation so that we can joyfully "serve the living God."

My tenth grade science teacher told us on the first day of class, "You're all a bunch of sophomores. Do you know what *sophomore* means? It means 'wise fool'—somebody who thinks he knows something when he really knows nothing. So I'm not going to expect much out of you." He got just what he expected. Coaches who tell their players that they can't make it get much less from them than coaches who say they can. Our struggle to please God will fail unless we know from the start that he is on our side, that condemnation is

30   Hebrews 9:13–14.

no longer part of his vocabulary as far as we are concerned. Because of the Cross, God's closeness no longer threatens, but rather inspires.

The Cross brings us closer to God than our Old Testament forebears could be. In their case, God inhabited the temple; in ours, he inhabits us:

> As you come to him, the living Stone—rejected by men but chosen by God and precious to him—you also, like living stones, are being built into a spiritual house to be a holy priesthood, offering spiritual sacrifices acceptable to God through Jesus Christ.[31]

We are God's permanent temple through Jesus Christ, both individually and corporately, thus making the old building (any building, for that matter) essentially obsolete.[32] We do not have to go to some "religious" place to be near God— the office, the kitchen, the bulldozer, even the ladies room will do. Nor do we have to seek the help of an officially or unofficially "religious" person to get through to him. For we are all priests—"a holy priesthood, offering spiritual sacrifices acceptable to God through Jesus Christ."

Consider the significance and privilege of belonging to God's "holy priesthood." It means that our prayers on behalf of our world and our friends—however untutored and weak—get through and have clout. It means that God hears and enjoys our worship, despite its many imperfections. It

---

31 1 Peter 2:4–5.

32 The destruction of the temple by Rome in A.D. 70 taught this great truth.

means that God accepts our service and makes it spiritually effective, despite our tangled motives.

Our priestly work derives all of its effectiveness and beauty from that of our High Priest and elder brother Jesus, who ceaselessly prays for us:

> Now there have been many of those priests, since death prevented them from continuing in office; but because Jesus lives forever, he has a permanent priesthood. Therefore he is able to save completely those who come to God through him, because he always lives to intercede for them.[33]

We enjoy God's presence and offer him acceptable sacrifices for one reason only: Jesus Christ keeps praying for us, applying his perfect sacrifice to our mixed motives, taking our weak, ignorant petitions and making them strong and acceptable. Daily he brings us into the throne room of the "judge who is God of all," and through his "sprinkled blood" makes our needs known. He does so with great understanding and power because he "in every respect has been tempted as we are, yet without sin," so that we may "with confidence draw near to the throne of grace, that we may receive mercy and find grace to help in time of need."[34]

Planned from the Start

Did the Old Testament promise really fail? Did God try out the temple and the priesthood and, finding them hope-

33   Hebrews 7:23–25.
34   Hebrews 4:15–16 RSV; 12:23–24 RSV.

lessly flawed, turn to something better? Of course not. Jesus came not to repudiate the temple, but to fulfill its deepest purpose. (His cleansing of it both honored the institution and symbolically enacted what the Cross would do for us.) God determined from the very beginning to restore a wandering race to fellowship with himself through the gift of his Son. God gave us the temple and the priestly system to help us understand Jesus Christ, the One who "tabernacled" among us, who lived, died, and rose for us, who lives in and with us, and who will pray us home to glory.

Questions for Discussion and Reflection

1. The early part of this chapter lists some of the ways in which we try to deal with a bad conscience. Discuss them and try to add to the list.
    a. Illustrate some of the "solutions" you just listed, either from your personal experience (if you are brave enough) or from human experience more generally.
    b. Consider David's response to Nathan in 2 Samuel 12:5–6 and Adam's response to God in Genesis 3:10, 12. Why did they respond as they did? How do we behave similarly?
2. Respond to the following statement: "God's wrath is not like ours. It is not mean, out of control, or partial. Rather, it is the fair and necessary expression of his goodness, a goodness that will not and cannot tolerate anything that is not good. A God who did not consistently and fairly judge evil would not be a God worth worshiping."

3. Have you ever felt anything akin to Isaiah's "Woe is me!" experience (Isaiah 6)? Try to recall the experience in some detail. Why were you "undone"?

4. List from Leviticus 1–7 some of the different kinds of sacrifices that the Old Testament priests supervised.

   a. Which were voluntary and which were required?

   b. Which were given entirely to God, and which were shared?

   c. What did each of the following sacrifices foreshadow in the life, death, and/or present ministry of Jesus Christ?

      • the burnt offering

      • the continual offering of incense in the temple

      • the sin offering and the fellowship offering

   d. Spend some time thanking Jesus Christ for his priestly work for you.

5. Outline the ceremonies on the annual Day of Atonement as set forth in Leviticus 16.

   a. What truths did the ceremonies teach?

   b. Imagine yourself watching the scapegoat ceremony (vv. 8, 20–22). What effect would it have had on you, particularly if you had recently done something you knew was wrong (see Psalm 103:12)?

6. Read the story of the dedication of the temple in 1 Kings 8:10–11.

   a. Why did God's cloud fill the place?

   b. What effect did that cloud have on the priests? Why?

7. Read the story of Uzzah in 1 Chronicles 13.

a. Why did God act as he did against Uzzah?

b. What effect did God's action have upon David?

c. How do you react to the story? Why?

8. Read Isaiah 1:11–17. Why did God hate Israel's sacrifices in Isaiah's day? What does this teach us?

9. Read Hebrews 12:18–29, where the author contrasts two different mountains (earthly Sinai and heavenly Zion/Jerusalem).

a. How do the mountains differ (list as many differences as you can find)? Why?

b. What does the difference mean for us (see vv. 28–29)?

10. How are we supposed to exercise our priesthood according to the following passages?

- Romans 12:1–2
- 1 Corinthians 6:18–20
- 2 Corinthians 6:14–16
- 1 Timothy 2:1–7 (Ephesians 6:18–20)
- Hebrews 13:15–16
- 1 Peter 2:9

11. John 17 describes Jesus' present prayer ministry for us. What does he pray for? Spend some time thanking him for those things and praying for them yourself.

Chapter 10

WHO WILL UNITE US?

I grew up with the Berlin Wall. When I was thirteen, a young man only five years my senior was shot to death while trying to escape over it to freedom. His repeated cries of "Help me" as he lay bleeding to death in no-man's-land still haunt me.

Although the wall no longer stands, it remains a fitting symbol of our times. Who among the utopians at the end of the nineteenth century (Marxist or otherwise) could have imagined the social destructiveness of the twentieth? The divisions among us have grown bloodier, more widespread, more systematic, and more callous. Two world wars introduced weaponry of unprecedented killing power (from the machine gun to the atomic bomb) and saw the end of the gentleman's code of warfare (where civilians are spared and prisoners are respected). State-sanctioned social engineering in the Soviet Union, Nazi Germany, South Africa, Cambodia, and many other places dispossessed, enslaved, and systematically murdered tens of millions. Terrorism (do-

145

mestic and international) came into vogue following World War II, marked by assassinations, hostage taking, suicide bombings, and public killings of innocent civilians.

Weary of conflict and reprieved by the collapse of Soviet communism, we reduced the level of international violence at the end of the twentieth century. But this has only made the problems at home more obvious. War in the city has tended to replace war between nations. Between 1953 and 1992, for example, the annual homicide total in Los Angeles County rose from 82 to 2512, though the population only doubled.[1] Tens of thousands of homeless children flock to the major cities of the world, where they beg, steal, kill, and are killed by one another and by the besieged citizenry. Racial, domestic, and drug-related violence, widespread and just below the surface, frustrates and endangers police constantly. Prisons in the United States are overcrowded, filled disproportionately with the poor and powerless, and they foster crime, rather than deter it. Marriages in our day fail at a rate of 50 percent, leaving angry children who often repeat the pattern.

Our times only emphasize the sad truth of human social history—we have never gotten along with each other very well, at any level. The problem began in Eden. When Adam disregarded God's command, he invited a mysterious and

---

1 Cited by David Barry in "Screen Violence: It's Killing Us," *Harvard Magazine,* November–December 1993, 38. Decreased violence in the latter half of the nineties came as a welcome relief, but I suspect that it was dependent upon the strong economy. Violence is always just below the surface, and racism seems as strong as ever.

powerful destruction into his marriage (and ultimately into all human relationships). The man who sang Eve's praise as "bone of my bones and flesh of my flesh" abruptly changed his tune to condemnation: "The woman you put here with me—she gave me some fruit from the tree, and I ate it."[2]

From that point on, tragic disintegration in human relations fills the pages of Scripture. Cain murders his brother and then refuses to be held accountable for it ("Am I my brother's keeper?"). Cain's descendant Lamech extols in song the murder of a man who wounded him. By the time of Noah, "the earth [is so] full of violence" that God determines to wipe it clean of humanity and start afresh with Noah's family. But even after the Flood's purging, the corrupt root remains. The human race endeavors to "make a name for [itself]" by building "a tower that reaches to the heavens." (Ironically, the only pursuit that now unites us is our effort to lay siege to the heavens!) The Lord judges this arrogance by confusing people's speech and scattering them "over the face of the whole earth." In the curse of Babel, God brings to full flower the social alienation that took root in Eden.[3]

The Need Created by the Fall

Thinkers, politicians, and activists of all sorts have striven through the ages to heal this brokenness. Thomas More, Karl Marx, Jean Jacques Rousseau, Martin Luther King, and countless others have dreamed, taught, and written about it. William Wilberforce fought for it in Parlia-

---

2 Genesis 2:23; 3:12.
3 Genesis 4:9, 23–24; 6:11; 11:4, 9.

ment, giving his life to the abolition of the British slave trade. We have seen this longing in the protests of European students against nuclear arms—and in the advocacy of them by hawkish Americans. We see it in the prayers of children that their parents will stop fighting. We see it in voter euphoria following an election and in voter bitterness over the failures of those they elected. We see it in the hype of benefit concerts aimed at alleviating world hunger and in the enthusiasm of an international missions convention. We want and need a better world—a place where justice, honesty, freedom, peace, compassion, and love reign universally. Our strategies may vary, but we want the same thing.

The Old Testament "Solution"

When God cursed the Serpent in Genesis 3:15, he promised to put enmity between him and the woman. Since Eve is the mother of us all, that promise meant in part the removal of Satan's destructive influence from the human race as a whole. With the calling of Abraham, we begin to see more clearly how God planned to fix things:

> The LORD had said to Abram, "Leave your country, your people and your Father's household and go to the land I will show you. I will make you into a great nation and I will bless you; I will make your name great, and you will be a blessing. I will bless those who bless you, and whoever curses you I will curse; and all peoples on earth will be blessed through you."[4]

4 Genesis 12:1–3.

Do you see that God's strategy for universal blessing had a political dimension? He planned to create a great nation from the descendants of Abraham and through that nation to bless "all peoples on earth."

From Genesis 12 to the end of the book, we see the early development of this strategy. God cares for Abraham and prospers him in the Promised Land. He miraculously gives Abraham a son, Isaac, who in turn fathers Jacob. Jacob, whose name God later changes to Israel, has twelve sons, each of whom becomes the patriarch of one of the twelve tribes of Israel. Brought to Egypt by Joseph, the family of Jacob prospers immensely until they begin to pose a threat to their hosts.

The work of Joseph in Egypt vividly demonstrates God's intention to bless the "peoples on earth" through Abraham's children. God prospers Potiphar's household because of Joseph. Later, life for an Egyptian jailer improves because of the Hebrew inmate in his jail. Later still, Joseph interprets Pharaoh's troubling dreams and manages the program that spares Egypt from famine and makes Pharaoh immensely rich.

Through Moses, God clarifies his vision of Israel's worldwide task:

> Now if you obey me fully and keep my covenant, then out of all nations you will be my treasured possession. Although the whole earth is mine, you will be for me a kingdom of priests and a holy nation.[5]

5 Exodus 19:5–6.

God will make the nation of Israel distinct among the nations of the world, set apart (or made "holy") by their ethical purity (they will obey his voice) and by their worship (they will serve as a kingdom of priests). In other words, they will model before the nations what it means both to be like God and to know him.

They will also model God's justice, executing his judgment upon nations that defy him:

> But be assured today that the LORD your God is the one who goes across ahead of you like a devouring fire. He will destroy them; he will subdue them before you. And you will drive them out and annihilate them quickly, as the LORD has promised you. . . . It is on account of the wickedness of these nations that the LORD is going to drive them out before you.[6]

Special Kings for a Special People

In keeping with his intention to make Israel distinctive, the Lord made it clear through Moses that Israel's kings should also be distinctive—of the highest caliber:

> When you enter the land the LORD your God is giving you and have taken possession of it and settled in it, and you say, "Let us set a king over us like all the nations around us," be sure to appoint over you the king the LORD your God chooses. He must be from among your own brothers. Do not place a foreigner

6 Deuteronomy 9:3–4.

over you, one who is not a brother Israelite. The king, moreover, must not acquire great numbers of horses for himself or make the people return to Egypt to get more of them, for the LORD has told you, "You are not to go back that way again." He must not take many wives, or his heart will be led astray. He must not accumulate large amounts of silver and gold. When he takes the throne of his kingdom, he is to write for himself on a scroll a copy of this law, taken from that of the priests, who are Levites. It is to be with him, and he is to read it all the days of his life so that he may learn to revere the LORD his God and follow carefully all the words of this law and these decrees and not consider himself better than his brothers and turn from the law to the right or to the left. Then he and his descendants will reign a long time over his kingdom in Israel.[7]

Israel, God's blessing to the world, must choose as her governors those of God's choosing, Hebrews of faith who refuse to look to other nations for help. The king of God's choice will guard his heart from the unbelief of foreign wives, he will resist the lure of riches, he will write God's law on his heart, and he will be careful to govern by it. He will rule in humility, not vaunting himself over his fellows. As a reward, he will reign long, and his line after him will continue for many years.

With the ascendancy of David, the shepherd king, it would seem that God's promise to Abraham is fast coming

7 Deuteronomy 17:14–20.

to its fulfillment. Despite his sin with Bathsheba, David remains the "man after God's own heart," and God blesses Israel under him. At his inauguration, God makes David an extraordinary promise: "Your house and your kingdom will endure forever before me; your throne will be established forever."[8]

That promise takes shape immediately in the reign of David's son Solomon. An ideal king in many ways, young Solomon does not ask God for "long life or riches or the life of [his] enemies," but rather for "an understanding mind to govern [God's] people." In return, God grants both wisdom and "riches and honor, so that no other king shall compare with you, all your days." A neighboring monarch, the queen of Sheba, visiting Solomon at the height of his reign, can barely find words to express her awe:

> I did not believe the reports until I came and my own eyes had seen it; and, behold, the half was not told me; your wisdom and prosperity surpass the report which I heard. Happy are your wives! Happy are these your servants, who continually stand before you and hear your wisdom!

We are told that Gentile monarchs and peoples from all over the known world made their pilgrimage to Jerusalem, seeking "audience with Solomon to hear the wisdom God had put in his heart."[9]

---

8 2 Samuel 7:16; see also Psalm 132:11–18.
9 1 Kings 3:5–14 RSV; 10:7–8 RSV, 24.

The promises made to Abraham, renewed with David in 1 Samuel 7, and seemingly fulfilled in the reign of Solomon, take on a special focus in the Psalms. In Psalm 2, God calls Israel's king his "son" and commissions him to overthrow in his name the evil nations of the world. God "laughs" at them:

> I have installed my King on Zion, my holy hill. . . .
> You will rule them with an iron scepter; you will dash them to pieces like pottery.

The psalmist extols this king's majesty, calling him "the fairest of the sons of men," full of gracious speech, victorious in his defense of justice and truth, and the object and source of joy and gladness among his people. He rules and blesses the nations by drawing forth from them a single song of adoration:

> I will perpetuate your memory through all generations; therefore the nations will praise you for ever and ever.[10]

What consolation and hope psalms like these must have brought to God's people as they used them in worship! They promised that God would raise up a Hebrew king to subdue and unite the whole earth in righteous, joyful, and eternal praise to himself.

The Historical Reality

Sadly, neither the people nor their kings live up to expectations. Disharmony and unrighteousness tend to char-

---

10   Psalms 2:6, 9; 45:2 RSV, 4, 17; see also Psalms 96; 110.

acterize God's "model" people from the beginning. Frustrated by Sarah's inability to bear children, Abraham decides to fulfill God's promise on his own by fathering a child through Sarah's maid, Hagar. Domestic havoc follows, resulting in Hagar's cruel expulsion into the wilderness. Matters worsen in the next generation. Isaac's twin sons become mortal enemies when Jacob (ably assisted by his conniving mother) swindles Esau out of both his birthright and his father's blessing. Abraham's great-grandchildren continue the pattern, sparing their brother Joseph's life only because selling him as a slave will turn them a profit.

One would hope that with their dramatic rescue from Egyptian bondage and their formal "incorporation" as God's beloved nation at Mount Sinai,[11] God's people might begin to be the lights God has called them to be. Instead, three days after crossing the Red Sea, the people begin the pattern of murmuring against Moses that continues until the great leader dies. On more than one occasion, they insinuate that God has planned all along to murder them in the desert. They have been wandering only two and a half months when they complain:

> If only we had died by the LORD's hand in Egypt! There we sat around pots of meat and ate all the food we wanted, but you have brought us out into this desert to starve this entire assembly to death.[12]

11 See Exodus 12; 19–20.
12 Exodus 16:3.

On at least four occasions, Israel's griping turns to outright rebellion: Miriam and Aaron question Moses' authority; the people vow to raise up their own captain to lead them back to Egypt; Korah, Dathan, and Abiram—together with 250 others—openly defy Moses' and Aaron's leadership; and—following Korah's supernatural defeat—the whole assembly of Israel rises against Moses.[13] On the outskirts of the Promised Land, Israel panics and refuses to enter, fearful of the "giants" who live there.

God keeps his word regardless, bringing his people into Canaan after forty years of chastening. His promise to bless those who bless Abraham and to curse those who curse him reaches new heights of fulfillment as one wicked regime after another falls before the wrath of Joshua and his army. True worship and the justice of God's holy law begin to replace idolatry, immorality, child sacrifice, and oppression in the region. Throughout Joshua's day, God's people labor together as one, and they vow on the eve of his death to remain faithful to their Master:

> Far be it from us to forsake the LORD to serve other gods! . . . The LORD drove out before us all the nations, including the Amorites, who lived in the land. We too will serve the LORD, because he is our God.[14]

But the patterns of unbelief run too deeply for this promise to last beyond a generation. The book of Judges

---

13 Numbers 16:41; see Numbers 12; 14; 16.

14 Joshua 24:16, 18.

vividly recounts the tragedy of a leaderless people repeatedly falling prey to the spiritual and political oppression of the nations around them: "In those days Israel had no king; everyone did as he saw fit."[15] Over and over again, the Lord hears their cry for deliverance and raises up a Deborah, or a Gideon, or a Samson to rescue them, but within a generation they routinely slip back into darkness. The sad history culminates in a bloody and ironic civil war in which the tribe of Benjamin suffers virtually the same fate that Ai did at the hands of Joshua.[16]

The conquest of the Promised Land should have issued in blessing to the world as God's righteous kingdom consolidated under his leadership. Instead, Israel became part of the very darkness that God had sent them to overcome. Called to subdue the nations to God's glory, Israel fell under their influence and in the end began to destroy themselves.

False Hopes

Light flickers from time to time in this darkness as God sends rescuers to his people. Jael kills Sisera, the commander of an oppressive king's army, paving the way for Israel's deliverance. Gideon tears down an idol in his hometown, precipitating an uprising that miraculously overthrows Midianite oppression. God gives Samson miraculously to an elderly couple and endows him with remarkable fighting power against the plundering Philistines.

---

15 Judges 17:6; 21:25; see also 18:1; 19:1.

16 See Judges 19–20. Note especially 20:29–48, where the description of Benjamin's destruction has many parallels to that of Ai in Joshua 8:9–27.

Some leaders—Moses, Joshua, Samuel, David, and Solomon, for example—fear God and teach Israel her proper role, fulfilling in many ways the Deuteronomic ideal. They love God's law (Moses and David actually write Scripture), they demonstrate remarkable humility ("Moses was the meekest man on earth"), and trust God in extreme difficulty (remember David's steadfast refusal to harm "the Lord's anointed"?).

Not even these great ones, however, fully pass the test. Moses resists God's call with one excuse after another, David seduces a subject and murders her husband, and Solomon turns to idolatry in his later years. The lesser leaders behave at times appallingly. Gideon makes an idol from the Midianite plunder and leads the people into its worship. Pride, lust, and revenge drive Samson more than his faith does. King Saul, the first great monarch, deliberately disobeys God and then vigorously denies his guilt.

Few kings following Solomon deserve mention, since most of them are thoroughly pagan. The few that stand for the truth—like Jehoshaphat, Uzziah, Hezekiah, and Josiah—almost invariably fall prey to pride or idolatry in the latter part of their reigns.[17] Those who manage to remain faithful invariably leave their painstaking reforms in the destructive hands of unbelieving successors.

Consider Josiah, one of the greatest reformers of Israel's sad history. Upon discovering "the Book of the Law," he repents wholeheartedly of the sins of his forebears. He renovates the temple, demolishes the pagan shrines that litter

17 See 2 Chronicles 17–21; 26; 29–32; 34–35.

the land, slaughters the pagan priests, and leads the people in a celebration of the Passover that surpasses anything like it since the day of the judges:

> Neither before nor after Josiah was there a king like him who turned to the LORD as he did—with all his heart and with all his soul and with all his strength, in accordance with all the Law of Moses.[18]

Sadly, all of this renewal falls away with his passing. His successor, Jehoahaz, does "evil in the eyes of the LORD, just as his fathers had done."[19] Within three months, Pharaoh Neco of Egypt deposes him and makes Judah his vassal.

The Failure of the Kingdom

The kingdom repeatedly falls short of expectations. God promised Abraham that he would bless "all the nations of the world" through him, and this never happens. For all its magnificence and wisdom, Solomon's reign benefits only its immediate neighbors. And it is tragically short-lived. A thousand years in the making, the golden age passes in a single generation. Civil war breaks out soon after Solomon's death, and the great nation divides, never again to be united, except once or twice through tenuous and self-serving treaties. The northern kingdom (called Samaria or Israel) falls to Assyria in 722 B.C., and its people are either killed or trans-

18 2 Kings 23:25; see v. 22.
19 2 Kings 23:32.

ported and absorbed into various cultures under Assyrian rule. Not too many years later, the Babylonians (also called Chaldeans) crush the southern kingdom and take its people into exile.[20]

Imagine yourself as a faithful Jew, watching in chains outside the walls as Chaldean brutes demolish Jerusalem and her temple. Three-fourths of your family has died during the siege, and those who survive the grueling transportation will soon live in a strange and spiritually hostile place. What has happened? Where is God? What has become of his high purpose for Israel? These questions plague you as much as your hunger and bereavement. (I suspect that many Jews asked similar questions in Hitler's day.) Habakkuk expresses your shock vividly:

> Look at the nations and watch—and be utterly amazed. For I am going to do something in your days that you would not believe, even if you were told. I am raising up the Babylonians, that ruthless and impetuous people, who sweep across the whole earth to seize dwelling places not their own. They are a feared and dreaded people; they are a law to themselves. . . . They fly like a vulture swooping to devour; they all come bent on violence. . . . They deride kings. . . . Then they sweep past like the wind and go on—guilty men, whose own strength is their god.[21]

---

20 See 2 Kings 17:1–18; 25:1–12.
21 Habakkuk 1:5–11.

God's people, your people, called by God "a kingdom of priests" and "a holy nation," are only one more in the Chaldeans' list of conquests. Called to bring truth and righteousness to a dark and cursed world, you are a mere statistic, overrun by the world that God sent you to deliver.

God's Deeper Purpose

Yet despite appearances, God's purposes have not failed:

Deep in unfathomable mines
Of never failing skill,
He treasures up his bright designs
And works his sovereign will.[22]

Ever our patient teacher, God knew that we must have this sad history to shock us out of our foolish self-reliance and prepare us for his deeper plan. Israel's unmitigated failure, despite God's presence and power, taught that a more profound intervention by God was still needed. He himself had to come as king, or he had to give to the world a king surpassing anything that human agency could produce. And God had so to capture the hearts of people that they would gladly heed the king he would choose.

We begin to see something of God's bright design in the Exile. In this seemingly hopeless foreign setting, God begins to conquer the nations inwardly—not by violence (as in

---

22 William Cowper, from "God Moves in a Mysterious Way" (1774), printed in *Rejoice in the Lord,* ed. Erik Routley (Grand Rapids: Eerdmans, 1985).

Joshua's day), but through the quiet courage of powerless exiles like Daniel and Esther, whose character and faith change the hearts of monarchs. Esther's sacrificial love for her people turns Artaxerxes' heart, thus averting Haman's murderous decree. Shadrach, Meshach, and Abednego's readiness to die rather than worship at Nebuchadnezzar's shrine leads to a miraculous deliverance so impressive that the proud monarch abandons his idolatry (at least for a time) and publicly praises their God:

> Praise be to the God of Shadrach, Meshach and Abednego, who has sent his angel and rescued his servants! They trusted in him and defied the king's command and were willing to give up their lives rather than serve or worship any god except their own God. Therefore I decree that the people of any nation or language who say anything against the God of Shadrach, Meshach and Abednego be cut into pieces and their houses be turned into piles of rubble, for no other god can save in this way.[23]

Most of us know the basic outline of the story of Daniel and the lion's den. Fewer have noted how deeply Daniel's character affects Darius, the king who reluctantly sentences him to death for worshiping God despite the decree forbidding it. The king cannot sleep on the night of Daniel's execution and rejoices at his friend's deliverance with a wonder-filled decree:

---

23   Daniel 3:28–29.

I issue a decree that in every part of my kingdom people must fear and reverence the God of Daniel. For he is the living God and he endures forever; his kingdom will not be destroyed, his dominion will never end. He rescues and he saves; he performs signs and wonders in the heavens and on the earth. He has rescued Daniel from the power of the lions.[24]

Imagine Daniel's delight upon hearing these words, not only because of their content, but because of their speaker: a foreign monarch and a personal friend, declaring Daniel's God to be king of all, and commanding that he should be worshiped.

The personal dimension in this story moves us and resonates with our evangelistic experiences. When the Christianized Roman Empire marched on the pagan lands around them, they would often drag their captives in chains through a river and declare them baptized and therefore Christians. Not so with the God of the Bible. His plan is neither to use force, nor to convert *en masse*. He builds his nation by taking people one at a time and using the faithfulness of his people, often demonstrated in great weakness, to conquer from the inside out.

The Prophets' Vision

What Esther and her fellow exiles saw in part, the prophets dreamed in full. As we have already noted, Psalms 2, 45, and 110 envision an international conquest by one

24   Daniel 6:26–27.

who is full of grace and justice. Daniel sees the same reality with great vividness, describing "one like a son of man, coming with the clouds of heaven" to "the Ancient of Days" to receive "authority, glory and sovereign power; all peoples, nations and men of every language" will worship him forever.[25] A man will govern the nations forever, and his subjects will submit to him, not by force, but willingly in joyful worship.

Isaiah rounds out the psalmists' vision of a cosmic battlefield and Daniel's vision of a cosmic throne room with his own vision of a cosmic city. God will so flood Jerusalem with his glory that the nations of the world will be irresistibly drawn to her—drawn as her willing servants, eager to rebuild her walls; drawn as her benefactors, eager to pour their wealth into her; drawn with their camels, their flocks, their gold and silver, and their forest wood. They will come by land and by sea, and they will come in countless numbers, so many in fact that the city gates will need to be kept open day and night to welcome them. Most significantly, they will come worshiping the Lord of Israel: their flocks will fill the altar of sacrifice, their "cypress, plane, and pine" will beautify the temple, and their praises will be the walls and the gates of the city. Violence, strife, oppression, and unrighteousness will disappear forever, for the Lord himself will be the perpetual light of the city.[26]

The character of this final kingdom will flow from the extraordinary character of its king. The conquering warrior of Psalm 24 has "clean hands and a pure heart." Isaiah

---

25   Daniel 7:13–14.

26   Isaiah 60 RSV.

names him "Wonderful Counselor" and "Prince of Peace." The "shoot . . . from the stump of Jesse" will delight in the fear of the Lord, will champion the poor and the meek, and will clothe himself in righteousness and faithfulness.[27] Most significantly, he will be a servant—first a servant of God and then a servant of God's people:

> Here is my servant, whom I uphold, my chosen one in whom I delight; I will put my Spirit on him and he will bring justice to the nations. He will not shout or cry out, or raise his voice in the streets. A bruised reed he will not break, and a smoldering wick he will not snuff out. In faithfulness he will bring forth justice. . . .
>
> The Spirit of the Sovereign LORD is on me, because the LORD has anointed me to preach good news to the poor. He has sent me to bind up the brokenhearted, to proclaim freedom for the captives and release from darkness for the prisoners. . . .
>
> See, my servant will act wisely; . . . so will he sprinkle many nations, and kings will shut their mouths because of him. . . . He was despised and rejected by men, a man of sorrows, and familiar with suffering. . . . He was despised, and we esteemed him not. Surely he took up our infirmities and carried our sorrows. . . . But he was pierced for our transgressions, he was crushed for our iniquities; the punishment that brought us peace was upon him, and by his wounds we are healed.[28]

27 See Isaiah 9:6; 11:1–5.
28 Isaiah 42:1–3; 61:1; 52:13–53:5.

He who brings justice to the world, the exalted and beloved Messiah of God, will dumbfound the kings of the earth. He will be tender with people. He will identify fully with the weak and needy, establishing his reign by entering fully into the sorrows of life—ugliness, rejection, loneliness, beatings, and death.

Throughout Israel's sad history, the Lord continued to reign, working out his plan despite appearances. What seemed to be an unmitigated disaster was all part of his deeper, Christ-centered, and worldwide purpose. As William Cowper wrote:

> Judge not the Lord by feeble sense,
> But trust him for his grace.
> Behind a frowning providence
> He hides a smiling face.
> His purposes shall ripen fast,
> Unfolding every hour:
> The bud may have a bitter taste,
> But sweet will be the flower.[29]

Jesus, the Long-Awaited King

For years, godly Simeon waited in Jerusalem for "the consolation of Israel." When Mary and Joseph presented their firstborn at the temple, he cried out,

> Sovereign Lord, as you have promised, you now dismiss your servant in peace. For my eyes have seen

---

29 William Cowper, from "God Moves in a Mysterious Way."

your salvation, which you have prepared in the sight of all people, a light for revelation to the Gentiles and for glory to your people Israel.[30]

Jesus is the Messiah of God, the promised King who satisfies our deepest longings for human harmony. Heaven rings even now with praise to God:

Hallelujah! For our Lord God Almighty reigns. Let us rejoice and be glad and give him glory!

The kingdom of the world has become the kingdom of our Lord and of his Christ, and he will reign for ever and ever.[31]

Jesus met the lineage requirements. He claimed Eve for his mother as fully as any of us. He was an Israelite, of the tribe of Judah, and a descendant of David. He also met the ethical standard, surpassing all men in grace, righteousness, and mercy, and obeying his heavenly Father consistently and wholeheartedly. During his earthly ministry, he declared, "My food is to do the will of him who sent me,"[32] even when that meant the cross. A servant to the end, he healed the sick, comforted the brokenhearted, preached the good news, and even raised the dead. Dead set against the use of physical force to secure his interests, he told Pe-

30 Luke 2:25, 29–32.
31 Revelation 11:15; 19:6.
32 John 4:34.

ter to put away his sword. He sought instead to advance his reign by words uttered in the power of the Holy Spirit. He was the ideal king of Deuteronomy 17, holding fast to the Scriptures, content in poverty, and ruling by self-effacing love. This King died to reconcile people around the world to God, and through that healing to reconcile them to each other:

> For he himself is our peace, who has made the two one and has destroyed the barrier, the dividing wall of hostility. . . . His purpose was to create in himself one new man out of the two, thus making peace, and in this one body to reconcile both of them to God through the cross, by which he put to death their hostility.[33]

God raised his Messiah from the dead, setting him at his right hand, and giving him

> the name that is above every name, that at the name of Jesus every knee should bow, in heaven and on earth and under the earth, and every tongue confess that Jesus Christ is Lord, to the glory of God the Father.[34]

From his place of authority, this King has poured out his Holy Spirit, the Spirit who makes Christ's reign effective by

33 Ephesians 2:14–16.
34 Philippians 2:9–11; see also Ephesians 1:20–23.

planting Christ's own goodness and love within people worldwide. That planting overwhelms the divisions among us, as evidenced so vividly on the first Pentecost:

> When the day of Pentecost came, they were all together in one place. Suddenly a sound like the blowing of a violent wind came from heaven and filled the whole house where they were sitting. . . . All of them were filled with the Holy Spirit and began to speak in other tongues as the Spirit enabled them. Now there were staying in Jerusalem God-fearing Jews from every nation under heaven. When they heard this sound, a crowd came together in bewilderment, because each one heard them speaking in his own language. Utterly amazed, they [declared], ". . . We hear them declaring the wonders of God in our own tongues!"[35]

The King of kings began to lift the curse of Babel that day, and he has been doing so ever since. He does this not by restoring to people everywhere a common language, but far more importantly by restoring a common love.

Isaiah declared, "Of the increase of his government and of peace there will be no end."[36] What could never have been true of David's reign, or Solomon's, or Josiah's, has become true of our Lord's. Injustice, abuse of power, and divisions still plague us, for the full revealing of Jesus' reign lies

35   Acts 2:1–7, 11.
36   Isaiah 9:7.

in the future, when he returns in glory to judge the living and the dead. But his kingdom has already come among us, is daily increasing, and will never pass away. We see it whenever we make peace with a Christian friend we have offended. We see it whenever a tyrant is overthrown, or police brutality is exposed and ended. We see it whenever a wanderer puts his trust in Jesus. We see it whenever Brazilian missionaries depart for China or Korean missionaries depart for the United States. We saw it when Martin Luther King linked arms with white clergymen along the highways of Alabama.

> To him who loves us and has freed us from our sins by his blood, and has made us to be a kingdom and priests to serve his God and Father—to him be glory and power for ever and ever! Amen.[37]

Questions for Discussion and Reflection

1. The account of the Fall and its aftermath in Genesis 3 teaches in part that the breach in our relationship with God leads to a breakdown in our relations with each other.
   a. Discuss how this message is played out in Genesis 3–11.
   b. Why does the one breakdown affect the other?
2. In 1887 a writer from New England named Thomas Bellamy wrote a popular novel imagining the world in A.D. 2000. He foresaw, among other things, uni-

---

37 Revelation 1:5–6.

versal peace, equality between races and classes, and no money, bankers, or lawyers.

    a. Discuss some of the great efforts at utopian social improvement that have been made over the last century (the various Marxist and socialist regimes, Germany in the 1930s, South Africa, the Great Society, Prohibition).

    b. What motivated these movements, and what went wrong?

3. Imagine yourself as a modern public official trying to live by the standards found in Deuteronomy 17:14–20.

    a. Which of the standards should you keep, which would be impossible, and which would be difficult?

    b. Spend some time praying for the leaders of your country.

4. When Jesus told Peter to put away his sword, he was indicating that the people of God must no longer try to form a theocracy (a political order that claims to represent the kingdom of God and which seeks to enforce that kingdom by human strength).

    a. Why did Jesus teach this?

    b. Does this mean that we should never seek to establish laws that promote Christian moral principles?

5. Read the story of Gideon (Judges 6–8).

    a. What does it teach about God's way of advancing his kingdom?

    b. Why do you suppose the story ends as it does (8:22–35), and what are we to learn from the ending?

6. Read Daniel 1 and 3 and note how God uses the exiles' faith and courage to influence their captors. What lessons can we learn from them as we seek to influence others for Jesus in our day?

7. Read the descriptions of God's chosen king in the following passages:
   - Psalm 2
   - Psalm 45
   - Isaiah 11:1–5
   - Isaiah 42:1–4
   - Isaiah 53
   - Isaiah 61:1–3

   a. Discuss how Jesus fulfills these descriptions, and spend some time thanking him.

8. Read the descriptions of God's promised kingdom in the following passages:
   - Isaiah 11:6–9
   - Isaiah 60
   - Revelation 21:1–8
   - Revelation 22:1–5

   a. Pray for that kingdom, giving thanks for the ways in which it has already appeared and asking that it will appear more fully.

Chapter 11

THE DEATH OF DEATH

That man is the product of causes which had no prevision of the end they were achieving; that his origins, his growth, his hopes and fears, his loves and his beliefs are but the outcome of accidental collocations of atoms: that no fire, no heroism, no intensity of thought and feeling, can preserve an individual life beyond the grave; that all the labor of the ages, all the devotion, all the inspiration, all the noonday brightness of human genius, are destined to extinction in the vast death of the solar system, and that the whole temple of man's achievement must inevitably be buried beneath the debris of a universe in ruins—all these things, if not quite beyond dispute, are yet so certain, that no philosophy which rejects them can hope to stand. Only within the scaffolding of these truths, only on the firm foundation of unyielding despair, can the soul's habitation henceforth be safely built. —Bertrand Russell

Death is a fact of life. It is the one appointment that none of us ever misses. From the tombs of the pharaohs to the "resurrection" of E.T., we have dreamed of ways to avoid the encounter. Dr. Russell tells us that we fool ourselves with such efforts. Not only will we die individually, but the memory of us and of all our accomplishments will ultimately be swept away in the catastrophe of a dying sun.

Death troubles us all. I first struggled with its starkness when, as a young teenager, I saw my grandfather, after whom I was named, pass away. My earnest prayers notwithstanding, I watched him gradually slip away from us until, in his final days, he seemed unable to recognize us. A veteran of World War I, he could speak only of "fighting the Boche."

Death troubles us as sex did the Victorians. We spend millions on cosmetics and physical fitness to forestall it. We support a modeling industry that pays vast sums to people who look young and healthy. Death bothers us so much that we cannot bring ourselves to mention it straightforwardly: so-and-so "passed away" yesterday, but will certainly "live on in our hearts."

The quality of life bothers us almost as much as its termination, revealing that, for many, this life is the only one we have. Consider how arguments about the quality of life tend to dominate so much thinking in social and medical ethics today. Or consider the overwhelming preoccupation with "the good life" in contemporary advertising. Or, for that matter, consider the array of books, seminars, and centers devoted to "realizing one's full potential" or generally making life more manageable—or even making life truly wondrous.

The Bible faces death honestly, acknowledging it as a mighty and inescapable sickness that afflicts everything, scarring nature with futility, making the earth hostile to people, and filling us as a result with lifelong fear.[1] Following our first rebellion, God cursed the ground, making it our mortal enemy:

> Cursed is the ground because of you; through painful toil you will eat of it all the days of your life. It will produce thorns and thistles for you, and you will eat the plants of the field. By the sweat of your brow you will eat your food until you return to the ground, since from it you were taken; for dust you are and to dust you will return.[2]

God's judgment makes life precarious and wearisome, a drudgery that we in the industrialized West know less about than the rest of the human race. The Bible explains life's shortness and pain quite simply. By refusing to honor God, we forfeited our relationship with God, the source of all life, and in so doing forfeited our claim to life itself:

> "Be appalled at this, O heavens, and shudder with great horror," declares the LORD. "My people have committed two sins: They have forsaken me, the spring of living water, and have dug their own cisterns, broken cisterns that cannot hold water."[3]

---

1   See Genesis 2:17; 3:17–19; Romans 8:19–23; Hebrews 2:15.

2   Genesis 3:17–19.

3   Jeremiah 2:12–13.

Adam chose to seek life by forsaking God's command, and as a result he lost it. God barred him from the Tree of Life and cast him out of the Garden. From that moment on, Genesis rings with the repeating phrase "and then he died"—a bell tolling for the race.[4]

The Old Testament "Solution" to the Problem of Death

Although Scripture speaks with painful honesty, it also provides hope. Intimations of a bright future occur within moments of Adam and Eve's sin. God stays his wrath, extending their lives and guaranteeing renewal. Moreover, he clothes them and promises that, despite the thorns and thistles, the earth will yield food. Unexpected and undeserved, these provisions hint at better things to come.

These better things begin to take shape when God promises to bless Abraham's children and through them the world.[5] The Lord details the blessing later through Moses:

> If you fully obey the LORD your God and carefully follow all his commands I give you today, the LORD your God will set you high above all the nations on earth. . . . You will be blessed in the city and blessed in the country. The fruit of your womb will be blessed, and the crops of your land and the young of your livestock—the calves of your herds and the lambs of your flocks. Your basket and your kneading trough

4 Genesis 5:5, 8, 11, 14, 17, etc.
5 Genesis 12:1–3.

will be blessed. You will be blessed when you come in and blessed when you go out. The LORD will grant that the enemies who rise up against you will be defeated. . . . The LORD will send a blessing on your barns and on everything you put your hand to. . . . The LORD will establish you as his holy people, as he promised you. . . . Then all the peoples on earth will see that you are called by the name of the LORD, and they will fear you. The LORD will grant you abundant prosperity . . . in the land he swore to your forefathers to give you. . . . You will lend to many nations but will borrow from none. The LORD will make you the head, not the tail. If you pay attention to the commands of the LORD your God that I give you this day and carefully follow them, you will always be at the top, never at the bottom.[6]

God promises blessing in every sphere of life—in national security, in the home, in the city, on the farm, in battle, and in domestic and international finance! And his promises extend beyond God's people to any who choose to live with them and call upon their God:

The alien living with you must be treated as one of your native-born. Love him as yourself, for you were aliens in Egypt.[7]

6 Deuteronomy 28:1–13. Cf. also Deuteronomy 33.
7 Leviticus 19:34; see also Leviticus 25:6; Numbers 35:15.

Choose Life

Where does all this "quality of life" come from? From the living God, who dwells with his people, not as a bureaucrat, but as a father and lover:

> Out of Egypt I called my son.

> Yea, I plighted my troth to you and entered into a covenant with you, says the Lord GOD, and you became mine.

> And I will be your God and you will be my people.[8]

But God's presence is a two-edged sword. It can mean protection and prosperity (to touch his people is to touch him), but it can also mean chastening if they disregard him:

> However, if you do not obey the LORD your God . . . all these curses will come upon you and overtake you: You will be cursed in the city and cursed in the country. Your basket and your kneading trough will be cursed. The fruit of your womb will be cursed, and the crops of your land, and the calves of your herds and the lambs of your flocks. . . . The LORD will

---

8 Darius the king rightly called Daniel the "servant of the living God" (Daniel 6:20), for God had declared, "There is no god besides me. I put to death and I bring to life, I have wounded and I will heal" (Deuteronomy 32:39). The texts cited are Hosea 11:1; Ezekiel 16:8 RSV; Jeremiah 7:23.

send on you . . . confusion and rebuke in everything you put your hand to, until you are destroyed. . . . The LORD will plague you with diseases until he has destroyed you from the land you are entering to possess. The LORD will strike you with . . . fever and inflammation, with scorching heat and drought, with blight and mildew. . . . The sky over your head will be bronze. . . . The LORD will cause you to be defeated before your enemies. . . . You will become a thing of horror to all the kingdoms on earth. . . . The LORD will afflict you with madness, blindness and confusion of mind. . . . You will be unsuccessful in everything you do; day after day you will be oppressed and robbed, with no one to rescue you. . . . Your sons and daughters will be given to another nation, and you will wear out your eyes watching for them day after day, powerless to lift a hand. A people that you do not know will eat what your land and labor produce. . . . The LORD will drive you and the king you set over you to a nation unknown to you or your fathers. There you will worship other gods, gods of wood and stone. . . . The alien who lives among you will rise above you. . . . He will lend to you, but you will not lend to him. He will be the head, but you will be the tail.[9]

These curses are indeed hair-raising. If they seem harsh, it may help to note that they merely reflect the downside of the great principle that life (and all its blessings) has only one source:

---

9   Deuteronomy 28:15–44; see also Deuteronomy 30:15–20.

> Every good endowment and every perfect gift is from above, coming down from the Father of lights with whom there is no variation or shadow due to change.[10]

To spurn that source, to replace the living God with gods of wood and stone, is to cut oneself off from him and to invite death.

We tell our teenagers, sometimes vividly, about the destructive effects of drug abuse, because we love them and do not want them to be snared. In the same way, God tells us the curses of the covenant. Driven by care, not cruelty, he warns us, concluding with a stirring plea:

> This day I call heaven and earth as witnesses against you that I have set before you life and death, blessings and curses. Now choose life, so that you and your children may live and that you may love the LORD your God, listen to his voice, and hold fast to him. For the LORD is your life.[11]

The Wisdom Literature repeatedly echoes these promised blessings and curses. As we saw in chapter 6, love of God's commandments guarantees "length of days . . . and abundant welfare." Wisdom, which begins with the fear of the Lord, is "a tree of life to those who lay hold of her." "He who finds me," says the Lord, "finds life." "The fruit of the righteous is a tree of life."[12]

---

10 James 1:17 RSV.

11 Deuteronomy 30:19–20.

12 Proverbs 3:1–2, 18 RSV; 8:35 RSV; 11:30 (see also 4:10–13; 9:11; 10:16; 14:27, 4).

How striking it is that the Tree of Life, from which God barred Adam, keeps cropping up in Proverbs. In effect, the Spirit of God is saying, "Do you want to go back to the Garden? Then worship me from your heart and walk in my ways."

Life-Enhancing Institutions

God ordered the social life of his people very kindly. For one thing, he scattered "cities of refuge" throughout the land.[13] If we had been living back then, and you accidentally killed my Aunt Alice, I would not have hesitated to dispose of you (or get an "avenger of blood" to do it for me). In fact, I might have done away with your wife and kids as well.[14] Cities of refuge put the brakes on this sort of thing by providing asylum for those who accidentally killed someone. The Lord slowed violence in other ways as well. He made all wanton and illegal killing a capital offense. In cases where a man's property (a runaway ox, for example) killed someone, he prescribed financial restitution (a "ransom for life") as an alternative to retaliation.[15]

Care for the poor and destitute figured prominently in the Lord's social legislation. Consider, for example, the sabbath year and the Jubilee Year, both set forth in Leviticus 25. Every seven years the land was to lie fallow. The people were

---

13   See Deuteronomy 19:1–7.

14   Some maintain that the *lex talionis* ("an eye for an eye") was given precisely to curb such excessive responses—so that, if you carelessly put out your neighbor's eye, the *most* he could exact in exchange was one eye.

15   Genesis 9:5–6; Exodus 21:28–32; Numbers 35:31; Deuteronomy 19:21.

to live off the proceeds of the previous year's harvest and whatever appeared of its own accord during the sabbath year itself. Such a rest for the land also meant a rest for the people—a special boon to servants, slaves, and laborers. On the Year of Jubilee (the fiftieth year), something even more remarkable was to happen. Anyone who in the course of the previous fifty years had to sell either his land or himself to survive was to be given back his land and/or his personal freedom. God intended by this to break cycles of poverty, on the one hand, and to hold at bay would-be robber barons, on the other. Imagine that—a redistribution of wealth twice every century!

But what about those who held no claim to the land— the priests (to whom no inheritance was ever given), the foreigners (who had no history of possession), and the orphans and widows (only men could own land)? The great "Jubilee shuffle" promised little benefit to them. But the Lord of life saw to their need as well:

> At the end of every three years, bring all the tithes of that year's produce and store it in your towns, so that the Levites (who have no allotment or inheritance of their own) and the aliens, the fatherless and the widows who live in your towns may come and eat and be satisfied, and so that the LORD your God may bless you in all the work of your hands.

Harvesting law also favored the poor, requiring landowners to leave the borders of their fields untouched so that the poor could glean there. Righteous Boaz kept this law, an obedience that led to his marriage to Ruth and made him the great-grandfather of King David.[16]

History Unfolds

For a time, God prospered his people remarkably. Abraham became extremely wealthy, and so did Jacob. In Joseph's time, the clan settled in fertile Goshen and grew so numerous that the king "who did not know about Joseph" tried unsuccessfully to kill off their baby boys.[17] Following the Exodus, they came through hard times to "a land flowing with milk and honey" (where a single cluster of grapes required two porters).[18] As we noted previously, Israel grew to such international prominence under David and Solomon that the Queen of Sheba could hardly speak:

> The report I heard in my own country about your achievements and your wisdom is true. But I did not believe these things until I came and saw with my own eyes. Indeed, not even half was told me; in wisdom and wealth you have far exceeded the report I heard. How happy your men must be! How happy your officials, who continually stand before you and hear your wisdom![19]

In the light of the blessings promised in Deuteronomy, these verses are very satisfying.

16 Deuteronomy 14:28–29 (see also 26:12–13); Ruth 2:2–3 (see 4:21–22).
17 Exodus 1:12: "But the more they were oppressed, the more they multiplied and spread."
18 Exodus 3:8; Numbers 13:23, 27.
19 1 Kings 10:1–9; see the whole of chapter 10.

But there were problems. The abundant life promised to Abraham in about 2000 B.C. and elaborated through Moses centuries later came slowly (it took a thousand years) and ended quickly. On their way to the golden age under Solomon, God's people suffered tyranny in Egypt (imagine living with a decree to destroy all your baby boys!), death in the wilderness (only two of Moses' generation got to enjoy the "land of milk and honey"), and a series of "pogroms" in the Promised Land. As we noted in the last chapter, civil war split the nation shortly after Solomon's death.

The problem was internal. Israel suffered because the people ignored God. They oppressed the poor, despite the prophets' warnings. They never kept the Jubilee and sabbath years (a halfhearted Jubilee effort during Zedekiah's reign failed miserably).[20] Consequently, the curses of Deuteronomy set in increasingly, until the nation collapsed entirely. Allowed miraculously to return after seventy years in exile, the Jewish remnant never again experienced the prosperity and freedom they knew under Solomon. While enjoying moments of independence from time to time, they remained essentially under the control of the Persians, the Greeks, and the Romans.

Much More Than a Political Problem

Nations and cultures die because people die. Even at their happiest moments as a nation, God's people felt the impact of this deepest curse. As the end of his full and pros-

---

20 See Jeremiah 34:8–16. Amos and Isaiah 58 represent well the prophetic denunciation of indifference to the needy.

perous life drew near, Jacob felt constrained to say, "My years have been few and difficult." How striking it is that the patriarch of a nation, living in the best portion of Egypt, should have described his life in this way.

Aging Moses shared Jacob's outlook:

> You sweep men away in the sleep of death; they are like the new grass of the morning—though in the morning it springs up new, by evening it is dry and withered. We are consumed by your anger and terrified by your indignation. You have set our iniquities before you, our secret sins in the light of your presence. All our days pass away under your wrath; we finish our years with a moan.

Moses lived life more fully than any of us. He saw and spoke with God "face to face," he was given and wrote down eternally binding words from the Almighty, he presided over the birth of a great and holy nation (a kind of Jonathan Edwards, George Washington, and Thomas Jefferson rolled into one), and he often witnessed and wielded the power of God in extraordinary ways. Nevertheless, this man of unparalleled experience, looking back on his life, saw mostly its brevity and darkness. He noted in particular the wrath of God. Evidenced in the universal judgment of death, God's anger makes all of life extremely fragile, "a mere breath," and an insubstantial "shadow."[21]

---

21 Jacob assesses his life in Genesis 47:9, and Moses in Psalm 90:5–9; see Psalm 39:4–6 RSV.

For many Old Testament saints, the realities of human experience caused God's life-enhancing promises to lose their appeal and even their credibility. Job suffered what appeared to be God's curse, despite his righteousness:

> Why is light given to those in misery, and life to the bitter in soul, to those who long for death that does not come, who search for it more than for hidden treasure, who are filled with gladness and rejoice when they reach the grave?

Life wore on the author of Ecclesiastes as profoundly as it did on Job. Abundance of knowledge, pleasure, riches, and power (virtually all the covenantal blessings) proved only that life "under the sun," even at its best, was hollow. He drew from the wealth of creation and discovered that creation offers only empty movement, endlessly repeating cycles. "Meaningless! Meaningless!" says the Teacher. "Everything is meaningless!"[22]

The Prophets' Dream

We reach for, but can never grasp, the fruit of the Tree of Life. Promise never matched reality in Old Testament history. The prophets took note and dreamed their dreams. Amos imagined agricultural fruitfulness far in excess of what was promised in Deuteronomy:

---

22 Job expresses his misery in Job 3:20–22 and elsewhere. The author of Ecclesiastes bemoans the vanity of life throughout his book, but particularly in 1:1–11 and 12:8.

"The days are coming," declares the LORD, "when the reaper will be overtaken by the plowman and the planter by the one treading grapes. New wine will drip from the mountains and flow from all the hills."

Isaiah envisioned unprecedented peace in the natural order:

The wolf will live with the lamb, the leopard will lie down with the goat, the calf and the lion and the yearling together; and a little child will lead them. The cow will feed with the bear, their young will lie down together, and the lion will eat straw like the ox. The infant will play near the hole of the cobra, and the young child put his hand into the viper's nest. They will neither harm nor destroy on all my holy mountain, for the earth will be full of the knowledge of the LORD as the waters cover the sea.

Zechariah and Ezekiel pictured a great day when a mighty river of life-giving waters would flow from Jerusalem into the whole world:

On that day living water will flow out from Jerusalem, half to the eastern sea and half to the western sea.

Isaiah often sang of "streams in the desert" causing life to spring from barren terrain:

For I will pour water on the thirsty land, and streams on the dry ground; I will pour out my

Spirit on your offspring, and my blessing on your descendants. They will spring up like grass in a meadow.

Isaiah envisioned a people so inwardly transformed that their joy and song would know no end:

And the ransomed of the LORD will return. They will enter Zion with singing; everlasting joy will crown their heads. Gladness and joy will overtake them, and sorrow and sighing will flee away.

These words, rooted in the hope of a return from Babylonian exile, depict something much deeper—a permanent return from inward exile to a life of joy and meaning.[23]

The prophetic vision gave a surprising prominence to the poor and needy. God would rescue them and endow them with power and glory. He would in fact turn the social order upside-down. Barren women would be given more children than those who marry fruitfully. The poor would be "seated with princes." The deaf and blind would see and hear while the ruthless would vanish. The needy would "lie down in safety," and the oppressor would be destroyed. Most shocking of all, an unattractive, lonely, condemned, and brutalized man would turn out to be the conquering and ruling Messiah.[24]

---

23 Isaiah 11:6–9; 35:10; 35:6–7 (see also 41:18); 44:3–4 (see also 12:3; 43:1); Amos 9:13; Zechariah 14:8 (see also Ezekiel 47).

24 Psalm 113:8; Isaiah 14:29–30; 29:18–20; 52:13–53:12; 54:1.

Jesus: the Bringer of Life

Born in poverty and yet declared to be the King, Jesus embodied what the prophets sought. When visiting his hometown synagogue, he identified himself with Isaiah's words:

> The Spirit of the Lord is on me, because he has anointed me to preach good news to the poor. He has sent me to proclaim freedom for the prisoners and recovery of sight for the blind, to release the oppressed, to proclaim the year of the Lord's favor.

With these words, Jesus proclaimed a Year of Jubilee (the meaning of "the year of [the Lord's] favor," or "the acceptable year [of the Lord]"), making himself its inaugurator. What sets this Jubilee apart is its comprehensiveness. Jesus will liberate us from every bondage—not simply the economic.

He substantiated this claim throughout his ministry, bringing life and renewal everywhere. Healing on the Sabbath despite the protests of the religious, he restored the essential meaning of that special day. He reminded us that the Sabbath is God's gift to us, given for our restoration, and not for the continuance of our bondage to sin and sickness. Jesus healed people physically, like the man born blind (John 9). He restored to her community the outcast with the flow of blood, taking care not only to heal her, but to declare her healing publicly. He cleansed the conscience, declaring forgiveness to the paralytic before healing him. And Jesus delivered from supernatural bonds the Gerasene demoniac, overthrowing the legion of spirits that possessed him.[25]

Jesus did more than improve the quality of life; he restored life itself. With "a loud voice" he rebuked death at Lazarus's tomb and his friend, dead four days, emerged at his command. In gentler but no less authoritative terms, he called a synagogue official's daughter and a destitute widow's son back from the grave. John's indication that "Jesus did many other signs . . . which are not written in this book" suggests that these were not the only cases.[26]

Jesus Christ championed life because he was life itself. He claimed to be the only way to the Father. He is the true and living water that quenches thirst deeply and forever. He is the bread of life, the true manna, that satisfies our hunger everlastingly. He is the light of the world, which removes spiritual blindness forever.[27]

Jesus saw himself not only as the source of life, but as the source of overwhelming life. He promised to give life and to give it "abundantly." I remember as a child selling Kool-Aid for five cents a cup at the roadside on hot summer days. Jesus offered the Samaritan woman not just a cup, but the whole company "on tap"—a living spring, gushing up continually with an endless supply of "eternal life." Standing in the temple, he used stronger language still: "He who believes in me, as the scripture has said, 'Out of his heart shall flow rivers of living water.'" Not just a spring, but a river. And

25 Mark 2:3–12; 3:4; 5; Luke 4:18–19 (Isaiah 61:1–2); Luke 8:48.

26 Mark 5:21–24, 35–43; Luke 7:11–17; John 11:43–44; 20:30 RSV.

27 John 4:10, 13–14; 6:35; 7:37–38; 9:5; 14:6.

not just a single river, but many—the Nile, the Jordan, and the Euphrates issuing in a vast flood of life.[28]

Echoing words we have already noted in the prophets, such language depicts life in immeasurable supply, far more deep and wide than anything known to God's ancient people. What did Jesus mean? And what does it mean for us? It means that Jesus brings God himself to us, not only as our companion in life's joys and trials, but as the wellspring of our lives. Jesus brings the living God to dwell *in* us, not just *with* us, and to dwell there forever.

The Mighty Baptizer

John the Baptist promised that the one coming after him would "baptize you with the Holy Spirit." Paul echoes this language when he describes the church as those who "by one Spirit" have been "baptized into one body." On the eve of his crucifixion, Jesus promised his disciples "another Counselor," calling him the Holy Spirit and promising that he would be "in" them. Jesus told a confused Pharisee named Nicodemus that unless he was "born anew" (or "from above") he would not enter or even see the reign of God in this life, summarizing his argument with the cryptic saying, "That which is born of the flesh is flesh, and that which is born of the Spirit is spirit." The apostle Paul describes his readers in Corinth as "a letter from Christ delivered by us, written not with ink but with the Spirit of the living God."[29]

---

28   John 4:14; 7:38 RSV; 10:10 RSV.

29   2 Corinthians 3:3 RSV; see Mark 1:8; John 3:1–8 RSV; John 14:15–17; 1 Corinthians 12:13 RSV.

These passages, and scores more like them in the New Testament, refer to the mysterious and life-changing ministry of the Holy Spirit. His work takes many forms, only some of which appear above. For our purposes, we can say that he is the "spring of water welling up to eternal life," of whom Jesus spoke. He is God the Spirit planted in us by the miracle of new birth. God the Father is in heaven, and God the Son lives in his glorified body at the right hand of the Father. God the Spirit brings God home to the human heart. And he is Christ's gift, earned at the cross and poured out at Pentecost.[30]

The Second Adam

All of God's promises of life come to fruition in Christ's gift of the Holy Spirit. But the Spirit did not fall until Pentecost, and Pentecost came only after Jesus' earthly ministry. In other words, Jesus had to be born, suffer, and die before he could give us the Spirit of life. To put it yet another way, Jesus earned our life through his suffering. Why? What does the Cross have to do with the Spirit? What does suffering death have to do with conferring life? Everything.

Twice in the New Testament, Paul refers to Jesus as the Second Adam. Here is one:

> For since death came through a man, the resurrection of the dead comes also through a man. For as in Adam all die, so in Christ all will be made alive.[31]

---

30 John 4:14. Peter's speech in Acts 2 makes this plain, as do Paul's words in Ephesians 4:7–8.

31 1 Corinthians 15:21–22; see also Romans 5:12–21.

Basic to the entire unfolding history of the Old Testament is the curse of Genesis 3. Adam and Eve forfeited life in the Garden—God barred them from the Tree of Life—and no temporary blessing or promises from God could undo this miserable fact. The Exodus, the manna in the wilderness, the Conquest, and even the golden age under King Solomon were like prison house film festivals—brief diversions from the grim reality of barbed wire, impenetrable walls, and gun-toting officers.

Adam was the problem. Somehow what he did had to be reversed. The catch-22 was that none of his offspring could pull it off, since they were infected with his mortal disease ("that which is born of the flesh is flesh"). To expect a son of Adam to rescue Adam's race from death would be like expecting a stillborn child to save the life of his bleeding mother. Only life gives life. A river cannot flow upstream. Israel's "life history," as related in this chapter, simply confirms the reality established in the Garden of Eden: sin kills the souls and inevitably the bodies of the human race.

Why do we celebrate Christmas with such fanfare? Because finally and for the first time a man was born from outside Adam's line. He was the son of Mary, and therefore truly human, but he was also uniquely the Son of God, and therefore free from the curse of inevitable sin and death. Jesus ran the Garden of Eden story a second time, with one profound difference. Not once did he partake of the forbidden fruit, with spectacular results.[32]

A British researcher recently reported the findings of an

---

32 Hebrews 4:15; see 5:7–10.

international study on health-care systems. At one point he commented wryly, "America seems to be the only nation that considers death to be an option." What is a silly and arrogant dream for Americans was true for Jesus. He did not have to die. Rather, he seized death as a wrestler seizes his opponent to pin him to the mat. And bringing to that conflict a flawless life, he won. C. S. Lewis masterfully describes the effect of that work in one of his children's stories:

> "It means," said Aslan, "that though the Witch knew the Deep Magic [that traitors must die for their treachery], there is a magic deeper still which she did not know. Her knowledge goes back only to the dawn of time. But if she could have looked a little further back, into the stillness and darkness before Time dawned, she would have read there a different incantation. She would have known that when a willing victim who had committed no treachery was killed in a traitor's stead, the Table would crack and Death itself would start working backwards."[33]

Jesus rose on Easter, proving his victory in history. To use Peter's triumphant words, "It was impossible for death to keep its hold on him."[34]

The Resurrection proclaims Jesus to be the Lord of

33 C. S. Lewis, *The Lion, the Witch, and the Wardrobe* (New York: Penguin Books, 1967), 148.
34 Acts 2:24.

life—and it guarantees that life for all who belong to him by faith.[35] With that new life comes the transforming Spirit. Here's how. To conquer death is to conquer sin (sin and death have been two sides of the same coin since Genesis 3). And to conquer sin—both its guilt and its power—is at last to make me fit for the indwelling Spirit. True, I continue to struggle with sin, but it can no longer condemn me, for I have died and risen with Christ. In the end, I will be rid of it altogether. The Holy Spirit can live in me because, through Christ, I have been declared holy (what we call justification) and will one day be made fully holy (what we call sanctification).[36]

If the president of the United States were coming for dinner, would you clean house? Did you bathe and comb your hair before your first really big date? Yes and yes. All through redemptive history, God has purposed to know us and to have us know him—as a husband and wife know each other. No fuller expression of that intimacy can be found than in the wonder of God indwelling us by his Spirit. But no reality has been more difficult to come by—since we are by nature so ill suited for it. At the cross, Jesus removed my

---

35 Paul develops this principle in 1 Corinthians 15, maintaining that Jesus' resurrection is the "firstfruits" of an inevitable harvest in which all believers share.

36 Romans 3:21–26 and 4:25 describe our justification through the Cross and the Resurrection. Romans 6:1–14 speaks of the breaking of sin's power through union with Christ in his death and resurrection. Second Corinthians 3:17–18 and 1 John 3:2–3 describe the process and final state of transformation.

filthy rags and gave me his own robes. As a result, on Pentecost he had somewhere to send his Spirit.

No More Futility

The Spirit of the risen Christ does more than indwell and renew me. The life-giving Spirit, who raised Jesus from the dead,[37] will one day raise us and, with us, the whole created order:

> The creation waits in eager expectation for the sons of God to be revealed. For the creation was subjected to frustration, not by its own choice, but by the will of the one who subjected it, in hope that the creation itself will be liberated from its bondage to decay and brought into the glorious freedom of the children of God. We know that the whole creation has been groaning as in the pains of childbirth right up to the present time. Not only so, but we ourselves, who have the firstfruits of the Spirit, groan inwardly as we wait eagerly for our adoption as sons, the redemption of our bodies.[38]

We wait eagerly for our "adoption"—by which Paul means resurrection—and, because of a mighty and mysterious linkage between us and the rest of creation, nature waits for us. Somehow, just as our death has caused nature's "bondage to decay", so our resurrection will cause its release. We could say that the cosmos will be swept up to glory on our coattails, even as we will be swept up on Jesus' coattails. And notice

37 Romans 1:4; 1 Corinthians 15:45.
38 Romans 8:19–23.

that all this bright harvest is the Spirit's work, the "first-fruits" of which we already enjoy.

God promised long life and prosperity in Canaan. Even at its best, the Old Testament fulfillment of these promises pales alongside what the New Testament tells us that God had in mind. In Christ, long life becomes eternal life, prosperity becomes unspeakable joy in the sin-free enjoyment of all good things, and the land becomes a renewed cosmos enjoyed through renewed senses. C. S. Lewis helps us imagine this unimaginable reality as only he can, describing the taste of fruit on an unfallen planet:

> [Ransom] had meant to extract the smallest, experimental sip, but the first taste put his caution all to flight. It was, of course, a taste, just as his hunger and thirst had been hunger and thirst. But then it was so different from every other taste that it seemed mere pedantry to call it a taste at all. It was like the discovery of a totally new genus of pleasures, something unheard of among men, out of all reckoning, beyond all covenant. For one draught of this on earth wars would be fought and nations betrayed. It could not be classified. He could never tell us, when he came back to the world of men, whether it was sharp or sweet, savory or voluptuous, creamy or piercing. "Not like that" was all he could ever say to such inquiries.[39]

Lewis's words echo the promise of the apostle Paul:

39   C. S. Lewis, *Perelandra* (London: Macmillan, 1967), 42.

No eye has seen, no ear has heard, no mind has conceived what God has prepared for those who love him.[40]

Already but Not Yet

Have we arrived yet? Is the real golden age upon us? Yes and no. Christ has come. The Holy Spirit has been poured out. The age for which the prophets longed has dawned. If we doubt this, we are not reading our New Testaments. Peter explains Pentecost by quoting from Joel's end-times prophecy. Elsewhere he reminds us that "his divine power has given us everything we need for life and godliness." Paul makes a similar claim, declaring, "If anyone is in Christ, he is a new creation; the old has gone, the new has come!" Above all people, Christians should be full of "living hope through the resurrection of Jesus Christ from the dead." We should know "inexpressible and glorious joy," for we live in the age for which the Old Testament Scriptures long.[41]

But we err if we say that we have fully arrived. Some teach that Jesus' promises of life guarantee healing now, if we would only believe. Some argue that prosperity is every Christian's birthright. Both experience and Scripture deny such claims. Like most Christians down through the ages, the apostles enjoyed very little materially. Paul lost everything and endured great hardship, including a painful malady from which he was never healed.[42] Imprisonment and

---

40   1 Corinthians 2:9.

41   Acts 2:14–21; 2 Corinthians 5:17; 1 Peter 1:3, 8; 2 Peter 1:3.

42   See 2 Corinthians 4:7–12; 6:3–10; 11:23–12:10; Philippians 3:4–7.

martyrdom greeted Peter and most of the apostles. If we think John's exile on Patmos was like a vacation on St. Croix, we are surely mistaken. The "health and wealth gospel," as some call it, is largely a North American phenomenon, as indeed it must be, since the North American economy alone can support the delusions it promotes.

The biblical language of "firstfruits" teaches and promises more than we currently have. When Paul says, "Now hope that is seen is not hope. For who hopes for what he sees?" he underscores how foolish it is to speak of Christian "hope" while simultaneously demanding that everything be fixed now. We still wait. But our waiting differs from that of the Old Testament saints, for "the guarantee of our inheritance," the Spirit of Christ, lives in us permanently.[43] It differs also because, thanks to what Christ has shown us through the apostles, we understand so much more:

> I no longer call you servants, because a servant does not know his master's business. Instead, I have called you friends, for everything that I learned from my Father I have made known to you.[44]

We know that "your labor in the Lord is not in vain" because he has triumphed and will triumph over sin and death.[45] Nevertheless, we are still waiting.

43 Romans 8:24 RSV (see also 1 Corinthians 15:23); Ephesians 1:14 RSV.
44 John 15:15; see also Ephesians 2:20; 3:4–6, where Paul speaks of the New Testament apostles and prophets as our foundation, the purveyors of truth long hidden.
45 This is the sense of 1 Corinthians 15:58.

Do you find from time to time that your life in Jesus is more wonderful than you can handle? If so, that is good—he promised as much. But it still cannot match what is coming:

> At present, if we are reborn in Christ, the spirit in us lives directly on God; but the mind, and still more the body, receives life from him at a thousand removes—through our ancestors, through our food, through the elements. The faint, far-off results of those energies which God's creative rapture implanted in matter when he made the worlds are what we now call physical pleasures; and even thus filtered, they are too much for our present management. What would it be to taste at the fountainhead that stream of which even these lower reaches prove so intoxicating? Yet that, I believe, is what lies before us. The whole man is to drink joy from the fountain of joy.[46]

A Final Word

The Christology of the Old Testament (the fancy phrase for the content of this book) should do more than heighten our appreciation for Scripture's marvelous coherence. It should stir us to love and worship. The Bible is an ancient love song, designed to win our hearts. I trust that as we have learned more fully how the Bible hangs together, we have also (and more importantly) heard the incomparable voice of the heavenly Bridegroom calling us away to himself. No voice is like his and no song compares to the one he sings to us in his Word:

---

46   C. S. Lewis, *The Weight of Glory* (Grand Rapids: Eerdmans, 1972), 14.

"In that day," declares the LORD, "you will call me 'my husband'; you will no longer call me 'my master.' . . . I will betroth you to me forever; I will betroth you in righteousness and justice, in love and compassion. I will betroth you in faithfulness, and you will acknowledge the LORD. . . . I will show my love to the one I called 'Not my loved one.' I will say to those called 'Not my people,' 'You are my people'; and they will say, 'You are my God.'"[47]

Questions for Discussion and Reflection

1. Reflect on the words of Bertrand Russell quoted at the beginning of this chapter.
   a. What in your own words is he saying?
   b. Do many think this way today?
2. When were you first keenly aware of the reality and inevitability of death?
   a. How did you deal with it?
3. How does death affect life, according to the following passages?
   - Genesis 3:17–19
   - Job 3:20–22
   - Psalm 90
   - Ecclesiastes 9:1–11
   - Romans 8:19–23
   - Hebrews 2:15
4. Deuteronomy 28:1–14 elaborates a gracious reversal at a national level of the curse found in Genesis

47 Hosea 2:16, 19–20, 23.

3:17–19. So do the numerous life-enhancing provisions of Old Testament social legislation, notably the sabbath years and the Jubilee Year, the cities of refuge, and the laws protecting orphans, widows, strangers, and priests. How would our world improve if this vision and the laws connected with it were implemented in contemporary life? Would it be possible?

5. Scripture teaches that "life" and "death" mean much more than biological existence and the absence of it. They are two separate spheres of reality, each of which encompasses a full range of experience. Try to define these two realities as the Bible defines them, illustrating them from Scripture.

6. Reflect on the following visions of life given by the prophets of the Old Testament. How do you imagine the prophets' contemporaries interpreted these visions?

- Psalm 16:7–11
- Psalm 23:6
- Psalm 113:8
- Isaiah 11:6–9
- Isaiah 12:3
- Isaiah 14:29–30
- Isaiah 29:18–20
- Isaiah 35:10
- Isaiah 44:3–5
- Isaiah 54:1
- Amos 9:13
- Zechariah 14:8

7. How in his person and work does Jesus Christ bring "life" to the following "deaths"?
   - human guilt
   - the power of sinful habits
   - social injustice and anarchy
   - human cruelty
   - meaninglessness
   - famine
   - physical death
   - violence
   - futility in nature

8. Why did the Cross and the Resurrection have to precede the pouring out of the life-giving Holy Spirit?

   a. How can the Holy Spirit live in me when I still continue to sin?

9. Central to our new life is "union with Christ," by which we understand that Christ is "in us" and we are "in Christ." What do the following passages teach about the blessings of our union with him?
   - John 14:15–17
   - John 17:26
   - Romans 5:1–2
   - Romans 6:1–14
   - Romans 8:1
   - Romans 8:12–17
   - 1 Corinthians 15:21–22
   - Ephesians 1:1–14
   - Colossians 1:27

   a. Summarize what it means to be "in Christ"?